Samurai and Cherry Blossom

Samurai and Cherry Blossom

*A Journey to Modern Japan and Along
the Ancient Tokaido*

David Scott

Illustrated by Steve Hardstaff

CENTURY

LONDON MELBOURNE AUCKLAND JOHANNESBURG

This book is for Edna Scott

First published in 1987 by Century Hutchinson Ltd,
Brookmount House, 62–65 Chandos Place, Covent Garden,
London WC2N 4NW

Century Hutchinson Australia Pty Ltd,
PO Box 496, 16–22 Church Street, Hawthorn, Victoria 3122,
Australia

Century Hutchinson New Zealand Ltd,
PO Box 40–086, Glenfield, Auckland 10,
New Zealand

Century Hutchinson South Africa Pty Ltd,
PO Box 337, Bergvlei 2012, South Africa

Set by Inforum Ltd, Portsmouth
Printed and bound in Great Britain
by The Guernsey Press Co Ltd,
Guernsey, Channel Islands

British Library Cataloguing in Publication Data

Scott, David, *1944–*
 Samurai and cherry blossom : a journey to
 modern Japan and along the ancient Tokaido.
 1. Japan – Description and travel –
 1945–
 I. Title
 915.2'0448   DS811

ISBN 0 7126 1692 6

Contents

Introduction

It is in their oscillation between beauty and ugliness, tenderness and violence, delicacy and coarseness, insularity and openness, and inventiveness and imitation that I find the source of my own curiosity and fascination for the Japanese and Japan. The title of this book, *Samurai and Cherry Blossom*, expresses for me both this union of extremes and the source of the book's inspiration.

To obtain the material I followed the ripening of the cherry blossom from the southernmost province of Japan northwards for over 1000 miles to Tokyo. The starting point of the journey was Okinawa, a Japanese island in the East China Sea. Okinawa is the birthplace of karate. The samurai of ancient Japan, from whom karate has inherited many of its traditions, had a nostalgic feeling for cherry blossom. They saw a connection between the beautiful but short life of the blossom and their own lives which could end at any moment.

The cherry blossom has been the national flower of Japan for many centuries. It grows and dies quickly, and the cherry trees are in full bloom for only a few days before the petals begin to fall. During those two or three days the Japanese gather in parties at traditional viewing sites to enjoy the blossom at its peak and to celebrate and mourn the coming and going of the seasons.

In Okinawa the cherry trees bloom in mid-March and the season then spreads gradually northwards, reaching Tokyo in mid- to late April and Hokkaido, in the far north, in mid-May.

I followed the season northwards not in fact to write about the cherry blossom festivals, but because it appealed to me as a plan for travelling through Japan in a way which would allow me to see the countryside at its most beautiful. The journey helped me to develop and clarify my own attitude to and satisfy my own curiosity about Japan and the Japanese, and to pursue further my interests in Zen, the martial arts, the samurai tradition, Hiroshige (the woodblock artist) and Japanese cuisine. These subjects appear in the book but not to the exclusion of other interesting topics.

This book is for the armchair traveller, the reader curious about contemporary and traditional Japanese society, and the prospective visitor or tourist to Japan. Some of the material presented here will, I hope, surprise the reader and clear up popular misconceptions about the Japanese. Some of it may also confirm their worst prejudices. Certainly my experiences in a Zen monastery may raise questions for Zen enthusiasts. Whatever is the case, I would like to say at the outset that I left Japan feeling very fond of the country and its people and respecting their way of life and values.

Getting There

I started my journey for Japan on a sunny early spring day by taking an afternoon train from Liverpool to London. This train is normally quiet but the one I took was busy with football supporters travelling to Watford to see Liverpool in the replay of the quarter final of the FA Cup. My carefully spread-out luggage, papers and coat unfortunately did not inhibit three other passengers from joining my foursome of seats. The journey was uneventful except for a trip to the buffet car. A bevy of Liverpool supporters, half drunk by the time the train had passed Crewe, decided that I had a resemblance to a character from the 'EastEnders'. They chanted his name as I went to and from the buffet car, an embarrassing experience for me and the other passengers. Getting off the train at Euston, I saw the same bunch shouting 'Liverpool! Liverpool!' as they left the station, cutting a swathe through scared commuters.

I boarded the flight for Bangkok at Heathrow, avoiding the long queues at the check-in for the economy class by going to the empty first-class desk. The stewardess booked me in after a small admonishment for not going to my rightful place in the economy line. The flight was to stop at Delhi en route and the lounge at the departure gate was full of Indian ladies in saris, which displayed their lovely roly-poly midriffs, carrying huge amounts of hand luggage. The Thai air hostesses were unexpectedly bossy. They did not fulfil any of my dreams of Eastern promise. Perhaps, I thought, a British Airways crew instructor had trained them.

On the plane I had requested an aisle seat. Here I could escape the claustrophobia of the inside position and be ready to head quickly for the exit in the event of a crash or a hijack. I had expected to be excited about this journey but instead felt rather flat. For an international businessman a flight to Bangkok on the way to Japan is a perfectly normal, probably boring, event. I thus rationalized my response as being unexceptional.

The plane took off in bright sunlight but within an hour the blinds had been drawn. They showed a film with a crackling soundtrack. It was as boring as aircraft food. I wanted to keep my seat light on but the distressed looks of other passengers persuaded me to turn it off. The film ended and the blinds were lifted to a black sky. We were flying into the night now, all the way to Bangkok.

At Delhi we were not allowed to get off but one could feel India outside. The cabin-cleaning crew worked on their hands and knees, not looking up and avoiding eye contact with the passengers.

We arrived at Bangkok airport at 6.30 a.m., but even at that early hour the atmosphere was hot and humid. Stepping out of the aircraft was like walking into a huge glasshouse. The airport was clean and the immigration checks efficient, but the ants on the stainless-steel desk of the passport control and in the urinals of the gents' toilets reminded me I was in Southeast Asia. The luggage took a long time to appear and we moved bays twice, trotting after a man who held a yellow plastic display board bearing our flight number above his head. Everybody fears losing their luggage on an air journey. I am acutely anxious about it since as a student I worked unloading luggage at Heathrow airport. There I saw how luggage can be mishandled and rifled.

Kristiaan, an Englishman with whom I had just written a book on Thai cooking, met me at the airport exit. He has lived in Thailand for over twenty years and earns his living as a writer, illustrator and graphic designer. He is married to a Thai woman and they have three children. Twenty years ago Kristiaan was also on his way to Japan when he arrived in Thailand for the first time. He never left.

My first impressions of Bangkok were of the intense heat and the wide main streets packed with cars and motorcycles driven without any seeming care for life or limb. It was so hot that when we got to Kris's house we huddled around a fan. It made a change from the fire I had sat in front of at home the night before I left. I was very tired and went to bed for a few hours. My metabolism decided it was the wrong time to sleep and I lay there wondering whether to go for a pee or ignore it and see if I dozed off.

Later that afternoon we went for a meal in a local Thai restaurant. It was delicious, particularly the cooked aubergine salad garnished with whole garlic cloves, shallots, diced shrimps and chopped chillies. Each mouthful of the salad was supposed to include some of each of the garnishings. The effect of this combination was so powerful, my tongue and the roof of my mouth popped and tingled.

I left Bangkok after a few days since the main reason for my journey was to visit Japan. I was rather sad to leave and would have enjoyed a trip to the north of the country and to a Thai holiday resort.

Leaving, I was reminded of Gilbert and George, the English painters, saying that on a visit to Bangkok they had slid from airport to hotel and back again. It is certainly a city that feels sensual and one that provides amply and cheaply for any sort of sexual proclivity. I saw blatant adverts for massage parlours in even the most respectable newspapers.

Back at Bangkok airport I came into contact for the first time with large groups of Japanese holidaymakers. They were mainly men on trips paid for by their companies. They travel to Bangkok by Japan airlines, stay in Japanese hotels and go into Japanese restaurants and bars. Their only input (and output) to the local economy is at the massage parlours.

Airports seem to bring the worst out in all people. The Japanese, despite their good manners at home, are particularly bad for pushing and shoving. This is not because of a personal animosity towards the people who get in the way. It is a result of their desire to move as one body, like an anthill with legs. Anything blocking their path is moved. Intruders are kept at bay by a judicious closing of ranks. To get across a column of Japanese travellers you have to be downright rude to a few members on the edge of the group. This should always be done with a smile. The reward is a surprised break in the ranks through which you can quickly pass. I should add that I find the Japanese to be a genuinely polite people. However, away from home they get nervous, insecure and disorientated, and act out of character.

My flight from Bangkok was to Taipei, in Taiwan. Here I was to catch a flight for the island of Okinawa in the East China Sea, my first stop in Japan. The climate of Taipei was a shock after Thailand. Despite being only a few hundred miles north of Bangkok, where it had been so sunny with a temperature of 100° F when I left, Taipei was cloudy, grey and miserable. The airport is large and extremely modern, but the visa formalities are long and tedious. The Taiwanese call Taiwan, confusingly, the Republic of China. They consider themselves to be in constant danger of attack by the mainland Chinese. Security is accordingly tight. I saw the entrance to a subterranean air-raid shelter in the arrival lounge. The Chinese officials were as quick as they could be in the circumstances. We even cracked a few jokes between us. I was surprised since my own humour is usually greeted by blank faces in the East.

The bus journey into the city was dark and I could see little. Once we arrived in town the traffic was dense and it took over an hour to travel less than a mile. The streets were congested with people, cars and takeaway-food stalls. On every wall hung neon signs and hoardings in huge Chinese characters. This was how I imagined Gerrard Street in Soho would look if you took an overdose of lysergic acid diethylamide. I booked into the YMCA hotel. The receptionist scolded me in a friendly manner for planning to spend only one day in Taiwan.

I went out to eat. All kinds of Chinese food were on sale, but I most enjoyed trying out the different kinds of steamed buns (*bau*). These were being rolled, cooked over charcoal braziers and sold at food stalls along the pavements. Later in the evening I went into what looked like a working man's café. I could not read the menu but was welcomed into the kitchen to point out what I wanted. After the meal I went back to the hotel. Country and Western music was being played through the sound system. It clashed with the noises outside like beancurd with a hamburger.

The next day Taipei was still overcast and cloudy, but the city was thronged with young people in fashionable Western clothes. People I spoke to were friendly and pleased to try a few words of English. I spent some time strolling around a few of the many parks, watching men and women practising various martial arts.

For a long time I studied two men performing the T'ai Chi 'Pushing Hands' exercise. They lightly touched the backs of their right wrists together as they circled their right arms. By pushing and yielding in a flowing and continuous fashion each tried to break the other's balance. Both were skilled at the

6

exercise and their relaxed stances and soft movements disguised intense concentration and physical strength.

In one park near Chiang Kai-shek's huge memorial building, which was impressive in size but void of any feeling, a small group of musicians played while two young girls sang in high-pitched voices. To my ears they sounded like tortured cats, but I enjoyed their unselfconscious public performances.

The city had an air of efficiency and endeavour. I wondered what the present balance of power in the world would be if Mao Tse-tung had been defeated and mainland China had become a nation of 800 million capitalists.

At the checkout lounge for the Okinawa flight I was glad to see some Okinawans. They had the dark, curly hair and large build that distinguish them from mainland Japanese. There were also several overweight, loud American military personnel on their way to the US bases in Okinawa. To me they seemed self-satisfied, insular and insensitive. But I was prejudiced since, once in the East, I begin to dislike other white faces, preferring Asian looks and valuing the anonymity my own whiteness and language bring me.

Okinawa

Okinawa, the birthplace of karate, is the main island of the Ryukyu archipelago, a group of Japanese subtropical islands in the East China Sea. They stretch south from Kyushu nearly all the way to Taiwan. Okinawa prefecture is the southernmost territory of Japan. It is the area of the first Cherry Blossom Festival of the year. In 1974–75 I had lived on Okinawa for a year, in a small town called Futenma, and trained with Master Uechi, one of the island's most respected karate instructors.

The first emperor of Japan was thought to be an Okinawan pirate called Jimmu Tennu. He led a force of men which invaded Kyushu in AD 200. From there he conquered all Japan. Every emperor since is said to be descended from his bloodline. Okinawa itself was occupied by the Chinese between the fourteenth and seventeenth centuries. It was then returned to the Japanese and remained under their control until Easter Sunday, 1945. On that day American forces successfully completed their invasion of the island. The invasion attempt had begun eighty-two days previously when five US divisions, supported by heavy naval and aerial bombardment, landed. The Japanese were well prepared. They were dug into the many caves and rock shelters that honeycomb the island. They fought fiercely and suicidally. Rather than surrender, kamikaze pilots crashed their planes into US ships, soldiers and civilians incarcerated themselves alive in caves, and mothers jumped off cliffs into the sea with their babies. By the day the Japanese finally accepted defeat 250,000 Japanese and 13,000 Americans had died. The United States occupied Okinawa until 1972 when it was handed back to the Japanese.

Okinawa is a popular resort for the Japanese. It is easy and cheap to get to and the weather is warm even in the winter. The

OLD TOKAIDO ROUTE ·····················

AUTHOR'S ROUTE ————————

TOKYO

MISHIMA

NAGOYA

SHIZUOKA

KYOTO

HAMAMATSU

MASUDA

TSUWANO

FUKUOKA

KUMAMOTO

KAGOSHIMA

post-war American occupation and the continuing presence of US military bases have produced a unique cultural mixture which is quite fascinating. It perhaps offers a foretaste of a future in which two of the world's most pervasive cultures, American and Japanese, develop side by side: Kentucky Fried Chicken parlours alongside *sushi* bars; conformity spiced with vulgar individuality; individual effort combined with company loyalty; hard business sense leavened with nostalgia and emotionalism. The marriage of the two cultures is exemplified in the mixed marriages common to the island: Western men with oriental women; masculine directness shares and competes with feminine subtlety.

The south of Okinawa, particularly around the capital Naha, is heavily developed and not pretty. However, the jumbled mixture of hotels, temples, McDonald's hamburger bars, ice-cream parlours, jogging GIs, Shinto shrines, Japanese tourists, strip joints, karate *dojos*, old men and women in kimonos, crop-headed marines and dense traffic fit comfortably together. It is easy to feel relaxed there.

The north of the island is a haven of small fishing and farming villages surrounded by sugar cane and pineapple fields and unspoilt beaches. Coral diving and tropical fishing are pursuits for the tourist. The locals prefer stronger fare for their leisure time. Dog fights, bullfights and mongoose and snake fights are popular. They also make a variety of flavoured, very potent *saké*. Two of the strongest are a *saké* matured in jarfuls of garlic cloves and a concoction known as snake juice. This is a *saké* matured in a wide-necked jar containing the coiled body of a dead, poisonous snake in the bottom. After ten years' maturation only the snake bones remain, the rest having dissolved in the *saké*. The drink is said to enhance stamina and sexual power. My experience was that a few glasses made me too drunk to move.

An unimportant but interesting outcome of the Japanese takeover in 1972 was that the Okinawans executed a midnight changeover from driving on the right to driving on the left. This aligned them with the mainland Japanese, who share with the British the internationally eccentric fashion of driving on the left.

I landed at Okinawa's Naha airport late on a Sunday evening in mid-March. We got off the plane and the Japanese passengers rushed for the customs building, eager to start their holidays. They rushed in a polite way that is uniquely Japanese. To join them puts one at risk of looking clumsy and aggressive. Instead I remained on the runway tarmac, pleased to be in Japan and enjoying the half-forgotten smells that foreign places hold in one's memory.

Outside the customs hall I met an American businessman called Brad. He was being met by his Japanese girlfriend. He offered me a lift to Futenma. His girlfriend arrived late and they argued because he apparently had not told her what flight he was travelling on. She was attractive, expensively dressed and spoke good English. He introduced me to her and we got into the car. From their conversation I gathered that she obviously expected more from the relationship than he was willing to give. He was based in Korea and jetted around Southeast Asia. He was vague about what his business was. Out of the window I could see Naha. It had changed considerably, obviously prospering under Japanese rule. Skyscrapers had been added to the skyline and there was more traffic on the roads.

I got out at Futenma. Here Master Uechi lives and has his *dojo*. It is called Shu-Bu-Kan, the House of the Refinement of the Martial Arts. The only hotel I could find with a vacancy sign was shabby. I seemed to be the only guest. My room was poorly lit and the single bedside lamp had a red bulb. There was a big double bed, a massive television set that did not work, a pile of comics, mainly of the bondage and sex types popular in Japan, and a door that did not lock. I paid in advance. The *obesan* (landlady) was, however, friendly and brought me tea and biscuits. I lay on the bed thinking what a strange hotel I was in. Then it dawned on me that it was a love hotel. In love hotels the rooms are hired out by the hour. They are used by courting couples, people having illicit affairs and marriage partners who want to make love out of earshot of children and in-laws. Most love hotels are luxurious and expensive. This one must have been at the bottom end of the market. Rooms are available overnight at reduced rates from about 10 p.m. onwards, hence my presence.

I went out to a bar to watch television. There I met a Filipino immigrant. We watched an episode of an old 'Avengers' serial together. It was set in an English country estate where an eccentric lord had recreated an African jungle and village. Steed and Emma, investigating the death of a local gamekeeper, were being attacked with voodoo. I had a job explaining to the Filipino that we had neither monkeys nor jungles in England.

The next morning I rang the secretary of the Uechi-Ryu Karate Association. He told me that an old friend of mine called Arbie wanted me to contact him. Arbie and I had met in Okinawa ten years previously. We had arrived at the same time to study karate with Master Uechi. Arbie is an American of Irish-Italian parents. He stayed on when I left Japan and three years later became the island karate champion. Now he is a successful businessman there and married to a Taiwanese girl. We had not been in touch for years, since Arbie does not like writing letters. I rang him and he invited me to stay with him and his wife, I-Shing. They have a comfortable house on a hill overlooking the Pacific Ocean.

I remembered Arbie as being generous, passionate, loyal, dogmatic, chauvinistic, quick-witted, and exceptionally strong and tough to train with. His years in Japan with his attractive and intelligent Chinese wife have changed him. He is now more sensitive and open, and kicks his training bag less viciously. He and I-Shing gave me a warm welcome and were exceptionally generous hosts.

My stay with them was marred only slightly by the American Armed Forces programmes we sometimes watched on television. Living in England it is easy to forget just how obsessed America is with Russia. Some of the news programmes and documentaries I watched went out of their way to generate anti-Russian feeling and to convey the impression that the Russians were sinister people intent on taking over the world. They were divisive, threatening and frightening programmes for any European to watch.

The following day I went to Master Uechi's *dojo* and on the way remembered how, ten years previously, Japan had seemed a magical place to me. It was where I held the hope of finding some spiritual understanding and peace. Now it was still special, but ordinary as well.

The large wooden shutters of the *dojo* were pulled back. I looked in at the polished, well-used wooden floor, the mirrors, the training equipment and the pictures of old karate men on the walls and felt some of the old excitement return.

In 1921 Crown Prince Hiroshito visited Okinawa and for the first time saw a demonstration of karate by some school-children. The demonstration was arranged by Gichin Funa-koshi, who was then the chief instructor of a karate school on the island. It was a great success and, building on this, Funa-koshi went to Tokyo in 1922 to demonstrate his karate skills. This was the start of karate in Japan and the beginning of its rapid spread around the world.

Karate in Okinawa developed in the nineteenth century from a fusion of Chinese martial arts brought by Okinawans from the Fukien province of mainland China and an indigenous Okinawan system of empty-hand fighting called *te*. *Te* and simple weapons systems using farming and fishing implements were developed in response to a decree by the Chinese invaders of Okinawa. They forbade the use by the islanders of swords and other orthodox weapons.

My own style of karate, Uechi-Ryu, was developed by the Okinawan Kanbun Uechi (1877–1945). He studied Chinese boxing at the Central Temple in Fukien province, China, where he was a student of the Chinese master Chou Tze-ho. After training with him for thirteen years, Kanbun Uechi re-turned to Japan. He did not teach karate initially, but became a farmer on the Japanese mainland, near Osaka. A young Okina-wan persuaded him to start teaching and soon he had enough pupils to open a school. He taught there for twenty-four years, but in 1944 was persuaded to return to Okinawa. Unfortu-nately he died a year later. His son, Kanei Uechi, became head of the style. He is still alive and teaches every day. Master Uechi is a shy, sweet man, much liked by children whom he enjoys teaching. His style of instruction gives equal importance to softness and hardness. I have never heard him raise his voice or tell a student off. Nevertheless, his *karateka* (karate stu-dents) regularly win the All-Okinawan Free Fighting Cham-pionship.

The classes at his *dojo* are relaxed and enjoyable. Karate on Okinawa is an everyday part of many people's lives. Training sessions do not have the obvious intensity and seriousness evident in Western and mainland Japanese schools. This some-times disappoints Western visitors, who expect tough training schedules and strict discipline. Okinawan *karateka* train steadily, year in, year out. They work on form, strength, body conditioning and speed. Out of this they naturally develop a beautiful style, which looks deceptively relaxed, and ex-tremely hard bodies with long, stretched muscles, which allow

13

fast and powerful punches and kicks. They spar with each other using power and speed but with sufficient skill and body conditioning, which has been developed over a long time, that neither partner is injured. The black belts at Master Uechi's club were exceptionally good and in comparison I felt weak.

The first time I visited his *dojo* on this trip Master Uechi was not sure he recognized me. I had left Okinawa as a quasi-hippie, with long hair and a beard. I now have neither. Once he realized who I was he gave me one of his warm but quiet smiles. He watched my *kata* (sequence of karate techniques) with the same concentration that he gives to all his students and gently pointed out my faults.

I no longer teach karate beginners. After ten years' teaching I have lost the enthusiasm and patience one needs to keep up despite the knowledge that most beginners will leave in the first year. Master Uechi has been instructing for over forty years, but one night at his *dojo* I saw him spend over half the class with two beginners, both under ten years old.

In the past Master Uechi ran training sessions five afternoons and five evenings a week but nowadays he has reduced this to three evenings. I trained with him on these nights and also visited other Uechi-Ryu *dojos* on the island. There are nowadays at least twenty to choose from. I began by going to Sensei Takamiyagi's classes. He is one of Master Uechi's most powerful and influential instructors. He is also an English teacher and thus most helpful in explaining details of style. Sensei Takamiyagi's personality is as strong as his karate technique and he dominates and possesses his students. They give him complete loyalty and commitment. I have a love–hate relationship with him since the sheer force of his character brings to the fore a basic cussedness in my own.

I also visited Sensei Yonamine's *dojo*. He concentrates his training on power and body conditioning. His students can do remarkable feats such as breaking lengths of 2 × 2 inch wood over their shins. Sensei Yonamine can be seen walking around the *dojo* conditioning his body with a baseball bat while he shouts instructions to the class. His party trick is to deflect blows from a baseball bat with his arms, legs and stomach. There is nothing magical in this, nor is it a manifestation of some secret Eastern wisdom. It is a demonstration only of the way that, after many years of hard, consistent and patient training, the body can be conditioned to withstand extraordinary punishment.

On my previous trip to Okinawa one of my favourite *dojos* to visit had been Sensei Shinjo's. He was one of the few men alive who had trained with Master Uechi's father. Sadly, he has now died. His *dojo* was small and very hot. On a good night the atmosphere in there was electric. Shinjo was like a tiger. He had glaring eyes and would roam around the *dojo* roaring encouragement to his students. After a class Shinjo would sometimes invite us to stay behind to eat with him and drink whisky. He loved whisky and after a few glasses would oscillate between melancholy and uproarious behaviour. He was quite a poor man and the *dojo* was also the family's dining room and a bedroom. At night all the five boys in the family slept there. They consequently lived and breathed karate. At the time Shinjo's eldest son, Kiyohide Shinjo, was a 5th Dan; he was the island's free-fighting champion at the age of twenty-three. He is tall, handsome, with wild eyes like his father, a mane of thick black hair and a thin but muscular body. He once visited America on a teaching trip and apparently inspired in the women students an enthusiasm for training not experienced by other instructors.

Sensei Shinjo and Kiyohide used to keep a Japanese fighting dog. They trained it by harnessing it to a small cart loaded with bricks and making it run up and down a local hill. Japanese fighting dogs look similar to bloodhounds but they have bigger haunches and shoulders, around which there is a lot of loose skin.

Shinjo once took me to a dog-fight meeting in which the main event was a match between the Okinawan and the mainland Japanese champions. The day we went was a national holiday and the streets were lined with food stalls and festooned with streamers and kites blowing in the wind. The dog fights took place on a caged circular stage surrounded by tiers of seats. Loud martial music which issued from crackly loudspeakers attached to the seating stands announced the start of each fight. The dogs are starved for two days before a contest and they reach the ring nasty and vicious. Dog handlers carried in contestants without ceremony by tail and collar. They slipped the dogs' leashes and then hurriedly climbed onto tall chairs perched on either side of the stage. Once the fights started the dogs, unexpectedly, did not bark and a short silence

15

marked the start of each bout. Then the crowd started to shout again. The dogs jockey for a grip on one another's shoulders. Once one gets a hold it hangs on with grim determination and tries to throw the other dog down. Occasionally one dog would go for the other's testicles. If this happened one of the men in the high chairs would jump down and spray the nose of the culprit with a stinging liquid. Such occasions were the only time I could discern any emotion in the eyes of the dogs.

The two dogs for the big fight were huge beasts. Each weighed in at around 150 kilos. They were carried into the ring wearing snow white collars the size of life belts, which were worn only by champion dogs. The fight promised to be a good one. The crowd was strongly partisan and most of the money was going on the Okinawan dog. Unfortunately the contest was boring. The two dogs were evenly matched and neither could win domination. Both tried illegal moves, such as nose or testicle biting. However, they were always quickly stopped by one of the judges. He jumped into the ring, lit a torn-up programme and stuck the flame under the penis of the attacker. A singed pecker was clearly not worth the other dog's ear, nose or testicle, and the offender quickly let go.

After twenty minutes of wrestling the Japanese dog flopped to the floor. The Okinawan dog tried to mount it but the man with the spraycan appeared. He put a stop to further humiliation for the defeated dog. The home champion had apparently won.

After several days on Okinawa I was invited, along with a visiting American black belt, to a party being given by one of the Uechi-Ryu instructors. We all met at Master Uechi's *dojo* and set off for the Ozeki Steak House in Koza city. Koza is a busy town with a red-light district. It is popular with the American marines. On pay nights long queues of them may be seen outside the brothels. Two chefs in tall hats greeted us at the door of the Ozeki and guided us to our tables. These had been arranged in a crescent shape and Master Uechi sat in the centre of the outside curve. Each table had set into it two stainless-steel, gas-fired hotplates. We were going to have *sukiyaki* (pronounced 'ski-yaki'), which is cooked at the table. Waitresses arrived and personally fitted each of us with an eating apron. It was rather like being back at nursery school again having a bib tied round my neck, but I did not mind. Next came hot napkins (*oshibori*), chopsticks and whisky.

Japanese men generally love whisky and, for some reason, particularly Johnny Walker. Master Uechi watched the proceedings with a benign smile and supped his Seven-Up.

The chefs, one to a table, arrived with trolleys loaded with the ingredients for our meal. Our chef melted butter directly onto one of the hotplates and laid on this a thin piece of steak for each person. While the meat was frying he deftly cut it into small pieces. On the adjacent hotplate he set about frying pre-cooked potato slices and chopped green peppers. As the steak cooked he flavoured it with squirts of sweet rice-wine vinegar and soya sauce and then tossed over it huge amounts of chopped garlic. In Japanese markets they sell peeled garlic cloves by weight – very useful for the professional cook. Just as the steak was cooked he seasoned the vegetables with toasted sesame seeds and more soya sauce. He served the steak and the vegetables onto our plates just as the waitresses appeared, perfectly on time, with beautiful black lacquered bowls of steaming boiled rice and clear soup delicately garnished with slices of red ginger cut into star shapes. Meanwhile the chef was starting to fry beansprouts, cabbage, cooked noodles and more steak.

After the meal serious drinking started and I slipped off to the lavatory. I walked over the thick straw *tatami* matted floor in my stocking feet, totally forgot to put on a pair of the slippers neatly parked in rows outside the lavatory, and went in. Returning to the table I was followed by a line of wet footprints. My faux pas was clear for all to see. Fortunately nobody showed they had noticed. The *tatami* matting quickly absorbed the evidence.

Everybody got steadily drunk, except for Master Uechi, who continued to sip his Seven-Up through a straw. Drunken men are not an uncommon sight in Japan. The Japanese get inebriated very easily. However, there are no social taboos attached to drunkenness, nor are Japanese drunks given to violent behaviour. The Japanese seem to me to be very sensible about fleshly pursuits such as sex and drink. They make a clear distinction between the needs of the spirit and those of the body and give both equal attention.

The American in the party got steadily drunker and louder. This was understandable since there is a strong moral imperative to get drunk if you are with a party of Japanese men. They expect it of you and your willingness to submit to the ritual is a mark, for them, of how much you trust them. It is a custom I steadfastly refused to follow on both my visits to Japan. On the mainland my stubbornness was normally greeted with silence and lack of understanding. Okinawans are more relaxed and minded less. The American who was grading for a higher rank the next day slapped me on the thigh and said how much he enjoyed being out on the town with some of the world's top karate men. He then turned to one of the instructors and said, 'Give me a real hard testing tomorrow. If I die, I die.' He repeated this request twice. It was obviously time for us to leave.

We left the Ozeki, took a side turning down an unpaved road and went into a local club. It was noisy and rowdy with lots of bar girls. We ordered Japanese beer and sat at the counter. As in all Japanese bars, even the most respectable, the hostess behind the bar tops up your glass as soon as you take a sip from it. This particular custom is really aggravating if you want a quiet drink, but it is unavoidable. A Japanese girl came over uninvited and sat down on a stool between us. She was big-breasted for a Japanese and obviously an attraction for the American 'boys' doing their duty in the Pacific. She told us in English that her name was Hot Pussy. The American ordered her a drink. My cue to leave was when she invited him to stroke the counterpart to her name. I left him to his chances.

Okinawa was hot and sunny and I enjoyed sunbathing each day, knowing it was winter back home. Hard training sessions in the evenings reduced by sense of self-indulgence. Okinawa is also a good place to begin a trip to Japan since the islanders are more cosmopolitan and less formal than mainland Japanese.

I had been there only two weeks when the rainy season started unexpectedly early. I decided to leave quickly and to travel to Kyushu, the southernmost of the three main islands of Japan.

My impressions of Japan and its people after two weeks were mainly good. I had an overriding sense of security and felt that the people were genuinely honest. I even left a push bike I had borrowed unlocked outside shops and the *dojo* with no fear of its being stolen. I saw no violence on the streets and in fact mugging, rape and burglary are relatively rare crimes in Japan. This experience of safety and honesty was refreshing and liberating for me after the violence and theft endemic to Liverpool and much of Britain. After two weeks in Japan I felt my neck and shoulder muscles slowly loosening off as I dropped my guard and started to relax. I now understand one of the reasons why the Japanese travelling abroad like to travel in groups. Leaving the security of Japan is frightening for them and they need one another's support to cope with it.

Businessmen and shopkeepers took pride in the speed and efficiency with which they served me. Everywhere the service was cheerful and friendly. I was welcomed into shops and restaurants when I arrived and given effusive goodbyes and thank-yous when I left. My initial response was to regard this as artificial, commercially inspired bonhomie. Either that or the Japanese were fooling themselves and believing all the cloying good-life propaganda put out on Japanese television and in magazine advertising. But with time I realized they genuinely and unselfconsciously enjoyed serving each other. For me this was a joyful contrast to the resentful attitude we have to service in Britain, where our behaviour demeans the value of our jobs and our self-respect, as well as making life for the customer miserable. The Japanese approach was demonstrated to me by my first visit to a Japanese petrol station. As soon as the car I was in stopped at the pumps a team of attendants ran across the forecourt to meet it. They were as well drilled as the mechanics at a Monte Carlo rally pit stop. One filled the tank, another cleaned the headlights, windscreen and mirrors, a third emptied the ashtrays and cleaned the mats, and a fourth took the money. On our way out onto a main road one of the team stopped the flow of traffic and guided us into the passing stream of cars. Finally he stood and waved goodbye!

It is, of course, this eagerness and enthusiasm to do business that is an important factor in Japanese commercial success in world markets. Another factor is the long-term view of Japanese businessmen. Competition is fierce in Japan, but it is founded on long-term objectives rather than quick-money schemes. First and foremost the customers must be provided with what they want and with the best service possible. Customer loyalty is developed and from this base the business and profits can grow.

Okinawa to Kyushu

At the domestic airport, Okinawa, the security guard operating the radar baggage scanner put my luggage on a tray before passing it through the machine. He handed it back to me on the tray and said thank you. He wore white gloves. The procedure made me feel more like a hotel guest than a suspect terrorist. The departure lounge was spacious with many seats and banks of television sets all showing the same quiz show. I went to the lavatory and almost crushed my face on the magic-eye-operated door when it failed to open. My nose and my confidence in Japanese technology were somewhat dented.

The pilot stood at the door of the plane and bowed to each passenger as he or she entered. An air hostess led me to my seat and brought me English-language magazines. On board there were several large video screens. The images on them were hardly visible because of the daylight but their presence was enough to comfort the passengers. Television is to the Japanese as a mother's breast to a baby. The seat belt and emergency-escape demonstrations and even the take-off itself were shown on the screens. Apparently a video camera was mounted in the nose of the plane. Had there been a crash on take-off we could have watched the run-up to our own deaths without leaving our seats.

The aircraft flew north over the Pacific Ocean towards Fukuoka, one of the main cities of Kyushu, the southernmost of the three main islands of Japan. As we approached the coast I could see in the distance the massive cone of the volcano Sakurajima, which is sited on its own broad patch of land across the bay from Kagoshima. It had once been an island but the lava flow of a recent major eruption now forms a causeway joining the volcano to the mainland. Sakurajima has been

active for many centuries and its southern peak still erupts. It quite regularly spews clouds of black ash into the air, covering Kagoshima in a fine coating of dust. I had been in the city on my last trip to Japan during an eruption and the ash fell like black snow. It collected in drifts along the shop fronts.

The British navy bombarded Kagoshima in 1863. It was in retaliation for the killing by warriors of the Satsuma clan of Kagoshima of a British subject. The lord of the Satsuma clan was so impressed with the British naval capabilities during the battle that afterwards he asked if he could send one of his men for training with the British navy. The man he sent was called Togo, and forty years later he became a national hero as admiral of the Japanese fleet that defeated the Russian Baltic fleet in the battle of Tsushima.

At the airport I phoned an English friend who lived in

21

Fukuoka. He was not in. I decided to leave the airport and take a bus into town. The bus driver wore a smart uniform and, like the street cleaners and baggage handlers, spotless white gloves. He made many announcements over his Tannoy system. I hoped they were not important since I could not understand a word. Nobody in the bus spoke any English and all the signs in the bus and in the streets were in Japanese characters. I decided to stay on board the bus until it reached the terminus, hoping it would be located in the middle of town.

Calculating the bus fare was simple. On boarding I took a ticket from a machine at the entrance. It recorded on it the number of the bus stop. At the front of the bus, above the driver, was a display board which electronically matched the bus stop number on the ticket with the current fare.

At each bus stop a disembodied recorded voice broadcast a thank-you to departing passengers and a welcome to those boarding. For me it was novel, but I wondered how the driver put up with it day in, day out. We stopped at a zebra crossing. Snatches of 'Coming Through the Rye' mysteriously filtered through the bus windows. I later discovered that this Scottish ballad was the safe-to-cross signal at all the pedestrian crossings in the city.

Fukuoka turned out to be a modern, bright city and larger than I had expected. I got off the bus not sure where I was in relation to my friend's address. I rang him again. One of his flatmates, a Japanese woman, who spoke a little English gave me directions. The bus terminus was adjacent to the underground train station I had to go to. I found an entrance to it and went down the steps, trying to make sense of all the Japanese signs. To my surprise the staircase led to a huge subterranean shopping mall. It was very busy, with shoppers, commuters, stores, restaurants, food stalls and even the basement of a ten-storey department store which I assumed rose up above the station. I got completely lost in the brightly lit underground streets.

Japan was beginning to feel like another planet. Suddenly, appearing like manna from heaven, I saw a sign in *romanji* (Roman alphabet) showing the way to the station platforms. There were no ticket offices, just lines of complicated ticket machines. I put some money in one, pressed the buttons that lit up, and obtained a ticket which allowed me to pass through the electronic barrier into the station. Fortunately there were only two platforms. On the walls clear maps printed in *kanji* and *romanji* made it easy to choose the right one for my destination. The platform area was modern, airy and light. Birdsong was being broadcast over the public address system. At the platform edge there was a series of raised metal studs. It was foot Braille for the blind. The pattern of the studs changed as the lip of the platform was approached. The train arrived. It was long, wide, smoke-free, air-conditioned and new.

Terry, my English friend, lives in a very small Japanese-style *tatami*-floored apartment with his three Japanese female business partners. Six feet three inches tall and wearing a large moustache, Terry is an oddity in a land of small, moustache-free men. He has lived and run a business in Fukuoka for ten years and speaks fluent, albeit colloquial and low-life, Japanese, much of which he learned from watching Japanese television. Terry is a double puzzle to the Japanese. In a land of entrenched nationalism and male chauvinism he is a *gaijin* (foreign) businessman and a part-time househusband. He and his female partners, one of whom is his ex-girlfriend, meet up for seven months of each year. They buy cloth in Osaka and have it made into their own specially designed scarves in Tokyo. Terry then sets up sales concessions with department store managers all over Kyushu. The girls go to the stores and model the scarves, which are designed to be worn in a variety of ways. While they do the selling Terry stays at home. He takes care of business matters in the morning, gets the shopping in the afternoon and makes a meal in the evening. The girls work long hours. They complain if dinner is not ready when they get home, especially if Terry does not cook rice. Japanese men friends find the set-up very difficult to comprehend. A man cooking for women! Terry's three female partners – Kumiko, Ayako and Mitsuko – are unique in Japanese society. They are women in their mid-thirties who have chosen to work for themselves, not to get married, nor to live within the family circle. For the months of the year when they are not working, they enjoy a leisurely existence in Tokyo. Terry returns to England to lead the life of a gentleman, betting on horses and watching cricket and Wimbledon.

The toilet and bathing areas in the apartment were ingenious and economic in their construction. The toilet closet was much too small to contain a washbasin but the cistern was designed to provide a hand-washing facility. The top of it was concave, rather than convex, with a plug hole in the centre. When the lavatory was flushed water issued from a tap over the cistern and ran down into it through the plug hole. Soap hung from a piece of string by the tap and you washed your hands as the cistern filled. The system saved water and space. Incidentally, Japanese lavatories are similar to the French type but are set into a raised platform rather than into the ground and one end of the pan is hooded. One squats facing this end. Western-style lavatories are now common in big cities but less so in country districts. I noticed that in places where they had been newly fitted, instructions on how to use them were pasted on the underside of the seat. I had taken it for granted that it was obvious how to use them, but I am told the lavatories at Heathrow airport are often misused by people unused to them.

For bathing there was a traditional Japanese hot tub. The tub itself was cube-shaped and deep enough to sit in up to one's neck. In Japanese households the tub is filled every evening. A small pump and heater fitted to the side circulates and heats the water until it is scalding hot. The bather sits outside the tub on a small stool and scoops water over him- or herself with a bowl, then washes and rinses off the soap. Now he or she climbs into the hot tub and soaks and relaxes. The next bather uses the same water and repeats the routine. This system means that the whole family needs only one bathful of water for bathing and each member can soak in clean water. Between baths an insulated cover is placed over the tub and it stays hot for a long time.

The Japanese find two Western habits difficult to comprehend. The first is that we wear shoes in the house and the second is that we bathe in our own dirty water.

The two main rooms in the apartment were the minimum size considered reasonable for a living space. Measured by the Japanese system, they were each six *tatami* mats large. *Tatami* mats have for centuries been of a fixed dimension. Nowadays space is so limited in big cities that in some new accommodation rooms are carpeted with mats smaller than the traditional size. The rooms, however, are still advertised as being six-mat size. This suits the developer and allows the buyers to describe their homes without losing face.

The rooms serve as living space during the day and as sleeping areas during the night. *Futon* mattresses and quilts are stored in cupboards in the rooms. They are unrolled at night and put away in the morning. This arrangement ensures that Japanese homes remain uncluttered. Furniture is often restricted to a television set, a low table and cushions.

One small observation to complete the domestic description: the washing machine operated only on cold water. The Japanese have never used hot water for washing clothes; even the machines in launderettes use cold.

The first night I arrived Terry and I sat drinking hot *saké*. I asked him what he liked about the Japanese. He told me they were more accepting than Westerners. They did not question themselves as much. What is the meaning of life, am I happy, sad, well, etc., are not questions they particularly reflect on. They are ambitious, but fatalistic about lack of success, naive, mutually supportive and helpful to slower companions. Some lead, some follow and there is no special merit in either role. The changes of the seasons, festivals or a new fashion are celebrated by everyone. Individuality is not admired and certainly not envied. I later noticed that even at events such as strike meetings, protest marches, punk gatherings or drunken company parties, ritual was more important than revolution. Traditional modes of behaviour are still deeply rooted in the Japanese national consciousness and they certainly bind society together.

The next day it was sunny and hot. I decided to go and sunbathe. I asked Kumiko if the Japanese sunbathed. She said, 'No, suntan does not suit a kimono.'

Later that day and over the next week I talked to the three girls about the place of women in Japanese society. They told me that the historical role of the Japanese woman was as the dutiful wife. Her job was to bring up her husband's children, look after his home and, among the poorer classes, help in his business. By law the home and children were his, not hers. Women from whatever background were expected to be obedient, humble and to complement their menfolk. To fail in these roles was to risk divorce. Men from the merchant and common classes were able to divorce their wives very easily. For a divorced woman life was very difficult and, rather than face the possibility, it was usually wiser for a woman to indulge and humour her husband. A samurai or high-ranking man could not divorce his wife so freely. He was in any case required by honour to maintain her according to her class and divorce was thus costly. He was, however, free to have as many

25

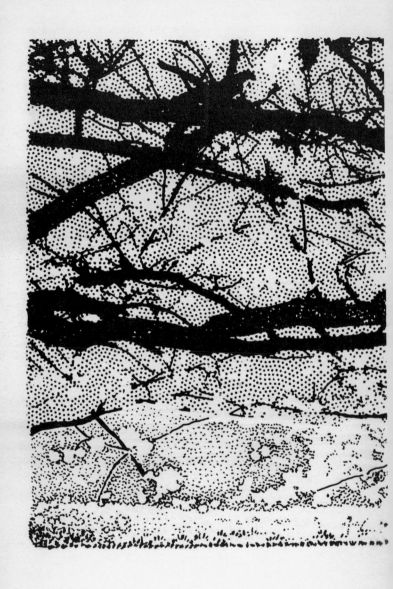

concubines as he could afford. An adulterous wife, on the other hand, took a chance with her life.

A well-brought-up young woman was taught to control her emotions, to be diligent in household duties and to be attractive and pleasing to men. She was trained to maintain a dutiful front. Jealousy in particular was considered to be ugly and egotistical. Even to this day in the Shinto marriage ceremony the bride wears on her head a *tsunokakushi*, a folded white cloth which symbolizes her intention of concealing the horns of jealousy.

In a traditional Japanese family boys were more important than girls. This attitude was rooted in accepted social values and in the Shinto practice of ancestor worship. The Shinto belief is that only males can carry on the family name. Sons and their wives have a duty to offer incense at their local shrine in honour of the dead ancestors of the son's parents, and to carry out other Shinto rituals related to family matters. Without a son in the family there would be no one to do this. The spirits of the dead parents and their ancestors would be offended. So important is this tradition that often families without a natural son will legally adopt a son-in-law to carry on the family name.

Attitudes towards girls are now changing in Japan, as they are all over the world, but in the past girls were brought up not to doubt the superior importance of their brothers. This was the training ground for their later obedience and subservience to their husbands. The boys also had their own pressures because of the system. The greatest was to get married. The family expected and demanded that sons married not only to continue the family name but also because a daughter-in-law provided support for the mother as she grew older.

Before the birth of her first baby, a daughter-in-law living with her husband's family had the lowest status in the family unit. At bathtimes the husband would use the tub first, then the father, then the mother and, last in line, the new wife. It was assumed that a daughter-in-law would do many of the domestic tasks. Once married, she became a closer relative than a blood daughter who was living with her husband's family. She was expected to be loyal and willing.

The daughter-in-law's power in the family increased as the years passed, however. Her first change in status came with the birth of her first boy child. Now she was able to give up some of her domestic duties and to devote her energy to his upbringing and to ensuring that he was a success in life. His success was important for her since through it she could exercise power in the family and the community. Even today mothers who use their children in games of social one-upmanship are quite common. They are called '*kyoiku* mamas' and can be seen, with their children, at stage-school doors, music academies, examination crammers, sports stadia and so on.

A mother's power in the household also increased as she and her husband got older. The husband, since he had all his needs catered for, became dependent on her. Thus although in public the older Japanese wife appeared to be humble and subordinate to her husband's needs, in private she may well have been the one who made the important family decisions.

In the past a boy child was indulged, appeased and protected from the world until he was six or seven years old. The same is still true, but nowadays girls are treated in this way as well. the child's whole world is centred around its mother. Even when going out the child will be strapped tightly to its mother's back. The child becomes totally dependent on its mother for all its emotional and physical needs. Individuality and independence are not qualities the mother actively encourages. The outcome, and I am not sure whether it is the one I would have expected, is that young Japanese children are usually orderly and modest. However, they totally identify with their mothers. This seems to be particularly true of boys and they often carry with them into adult life a deep nostalgia for their early years. A clichéd image in Japanese stories and theatre is that of a man carrying his old mother around on his back. The reverence for mothers in the male psyche goes deeper than that, though. Katsu Shintaro, a well-known Japanese actor, received much respectful publicity when he publicly kissed his mother's genitals at her funeral! Because of this nostalgia the ideal wife for most Japanese men is one who will mother him. In fact the word *kachan*, which means 'mummy', is sometimes used by men as a term of affection for their wives (as it is in Britain as well).

The idyllic life of the child ends when it reaches the school starting age of six. Suddenly, from being the centre of its mother's world and the most important being in the universe, it is thrust into the teeming world of school. Here the child has to learn to recognize the equal rights of all the other human beings who surround it. It has to learn to conform and at the same time to do well and stand out, a difficult and traumatic experience that often produces a schism in the Japanese personality. This manifests itself in the bewildering, to a Westerner anyway, Japanese ability to alternate between states of ego mania and passive conformity.

In Japan today women are in charge of household finances. The husband will give the wife his wage packet. She will give him pocketmoney. She pays the bills. At a restaurant after a family meal, the wife will pick up the bill and pay it. During the meal she will also serve the rice, pour the tea, order the beer for her husband and keep his glass topped up. She will do this unselfconsciously, almost as a right. He will accept it in the same manner. I was once treated in the same way by two young women I had never met before, with whom I shared a hotel table.

The place of women in modern Japanese society is complicated and difficult to judge out of the context of Japanese values. It is also changing. Traditional attitudes and customs such as those I have discussed are still important, but they are being modified by ideas from the women's movement and by changes in Japanese society as a whole.

Despite what I had read about Japanese women being downtrodden, my own experience was different. The impression I received, just walking around, meeting people, going into shops, asking the way and so on, was that the women were, if anything, more likely to be cheerful, bright and confident than the men. Teenage girls are naive and innocent compared with their Western counterparts but as a group they seemed to me to be the people who are enjoying themselves most in Japanese society. It is quite correct, however, that Japanese women have very little political or commercial power except as voters and consumers.

How women themselves feel about their roles in modern Japan depends, as one would expect, on which age group is asked.

Elderly women, who were taught that the place of the woman was in the home and that their duty was to obey the male head of the household, either father or husband, tend to think radical changes in women's attitudes will lead to a breakdown in society. They obviously take this view from the standpoint of their own experience. In many cases, as discussed earlier, in spite of appearances to the contrary, they and not their husbands are in fact the heads of their households.

Middle-aged women with reactionary husbands on the one side and daughters who expect equal rights to their brothers on the other are caught in the middle. Some try to maintain old standards while others welcome the changes and the greater freedom they bring. The latter are responsible for a new Japanese phenomenon, late divorce.

The husband retires and is now at home every day. He expects to be looked after. But during the years after the children had left home, when he was still working and they were financially secure, his wife developed interests and friends outside the home. His new presence brings an unwanted change to her life. On the other hand, he has devoted his life to the company and has not cultivated other interests. He wants companionship and mothering. She no longer wants to give either. A divorce results. It is most painful for the husband. He has to start looking after himself for the first time in his life.

Young married women without career ambitions are the group perhaps most confused about their role in modern Japan. Their homes are easy to run with many labour-saving devices. Also their children and husbands are out at school and work for long hours. They have more freedom, and money with which to enjoy it, than their mothers had. However, they may in fact want more to do and to see more of their husbands and children. They feel lonely and are bored with being at home all day. Some solve the problem by taking part-time jobs, others by studying. Traditional Japanese arts like flower arranging and the tea ceremony are nowadays experiencing a new surge of interest. Nevertheless some women in this group would prefer a traditional role and are unable to enjoy their new freedom.

Young unmarried Japanese women are the group who most clearly enjoy the newfound freedom of women in Japan. No longer are they treated as inferiors at home or in the school and, although they do not have equal opportunities in the work place, employment with good wages is assured. They are a readily defined consumer group with money to spend, and as such they are a prime target for magazines, advertising and media attention of all kinds. This has produced a generation of young women who are more sophisticated, self-aware and confident than their mothers were at the same age. Young Japanese women also travel more, both at home and abroad, than do their male counterparts. Because of this, they tend to be less insular than men.

One paradoxical outcome of this new selfconfidence in young women is that it is giving them the security to look again at traditional values and to choose them if they so wish. Arranged marriages are being freshly viewed as a legitimate avenue for finding a husband of the right education and income. Preparatory courses for traditional marriage skills (*hanayome shugyo*) such as cooking and calligraphy are becoming popular again. Even living with the in-laws is once more being discussed as a positive step for a young couple. Property is expensive and space is short. To live in the husband's family home offers a young couple the chance of saving money and of having more living space. Also as nowadays the wife can go out to work, she is no longer at home all day at the beck and call of her mother-in-law.

The return by some young women to traditional customs is not a return to being downtrodden wives. It is more a recognition of the practical worth of some old ideas in a society that is undergoing constant change.

Career women and feminists are those most dissatisfied with the rate of change in women's rights in Japan. Despite the fact that women make up 40 per cent of the Japanese workforce, most hold low-status jobs. Only a tiny minority of women ever obtain managerial or executive positions. In the postal service, the police force and local government offices exceptionally few women are employed at all. Take-home pay for women tends to be around 60 per cent of that of a man in the same job. The best-paid and most prestigious section of the workforce is male.

Equal-opportunity laws do exist in Japan, but there are no legal penalties for not obeying them. Employment laws designed to protect women from working long hours are also mentioned by many companies as their main reason for not promoting more women. However, some women wish to retain these laws to save themselves from the very long working hours and social pressures suffered by company men. Many young women want nothing to do with the company rat race. They prefer their freedom and the time it gives for personal development to the questionable advantage of a company career.

For those women who want careers, attitudes to work and women are slowly changing. However, the biggest obstacle to real equal opportunity is the attitude of ordinary Japanese men and women. In a recent survey the majority of both sexes accepted the correctness of lower status and pay for women. This was because they expected them to leave their jobs to get married and bring up a family.

Career women are still thought to be unfeminine. It is often women as well as men who resent or despise them for their ambition. Japanese feminists argue that women in Japan are second-class citizens, and that they are treated as objects rather than as human beings. There is much, apart from discrimination at work, to support their case, but the matter is complicated. Feminists also tend to ignore the growing confidence and freedom of young Japanese women.

To support their argument it can be said quite definitely that Japanese men in their hearts do not respect women as equals. This is shown in the way they instinctively treat them on a day-to-day basis. It is an attitude sustained by myriad social and linguistic traditions. That they see women as sex objects is clearly shown in the way that women are portrayed in magazines, comics and films. One of the true shocks to a Westerner visiting Japan is to flick through the sexy comic books sold everywhere and avidly read by both children and adults. The format is always the same. The back section is given over to one or two glossy nude female pinups. This is followed by a centre picture story in which the woman heroine undergoes all sorts of sadistic sexual humiliations at the hands of some evil pervert or monster. The only thing to be said in defence of the reading of these comics is that neither Japanese men nor women seem to relate to them in a way that affects their real lives. I am not sure what children think of them but they do not seem to be embarrassed or surprised by what they see.

Against the feminist argument, and surprisingly in view of the comics, there is very little sexual violence towards women in Japan. Compared to advanced Western nations Japan is a haven of freedom for women in terms of safety from male assault. Rape is almost unknown. Women are able to move around at any time of the day or night without fear of violence or theft.

The Japanese women I met did not think of themselves as second-class citizens. To imagine that they are is more likely to be a problem for Japanese men rather than for women, a problem that limits the men more than the women.

One final note on this subject. Japanese women now have a longer life expectancy than any other group of people in the modern industrialized nations.

During the time I was in Fukuoka I saw two surveys in the English-language newspaper, the *Japan Times*. One was on the young Japanese woman's ideal of masculinity and the other on her views about the ideal husband.

According to the surveys, the women preferred: an athletic, outdoor type with average intelligence to a sharp-witted but pale-faced man; a man of few words who speaks with substance to a smooth talker with little substance; a trim fellow in his thirties to a young but stout man; a man who is kind and sensitive but not very interesting or humorous to an amusing and upbeat one who is sometimes insensitive; a decisive but careless man to a methodical but indecisive one; a poor but self-reliant man to a wealthy, spoiled one; a resolute man who is not handsome to a handsome man who is fickle; an ambitious but not wealthy man to a rich man with only modest ambitions; and a generous man who lacks good fashion sense to a miser with good style. The last two preferences were closely run. Money and style are as important in Japan as elsewhere.

The ideal musculine man was not necessarily the ideal husband in the minds of the young Japanese women. The consensus of opinion on the details of the ideal husband were as follows: he should be four or five years older than his spouse and 6–8 inches taller; a salaried worker in either a technical or a government position earning about £14,000 a year; his most obvious qualities would be sensitivity and kindness; he would not have been married before and he would live separately from his parents.

Apart from meeting Terry, Fukuoka was of specific interest to me on another count. As an ancient trading port it was the site of the first landing of Khublai Khan's fleets in his invasion attempts on Japan. The tales of the Mongols' battles with Japan are fascinating; they are also the source of the name given to the suicide pilots of the second World War, 'Kamikaze'.

The story begins in the late thirteenth century when the then Great Khan of the Mongols, Khublai, grandson of Ghengis

Khan, sent an ambassador to Japan. He carried a diplomatic note recommending that relations with China, which was then part of the Mongol Empire, should be improved. The note was addressed to the 'King of Japan, the ruler of a small country'. From this the Japanese assumed they were meant to recognize the khan as a superior ruler. The ambassador was sent back without a reply. Other ambassadors followed. They suffered the same fate.

In response the Mongols decided to invade Japan. In 1274 an armada of 450 ships carrying 15,000 Mongol warriors set sail from Korea. They landed near Fukuoka on the north coast of Kyushu. At the time Japanese samurai believed that Mongols were half-witted barbarians who would be no match for them. The Mongols thought the Japanese were a race of midgets who could be easily overrun. Both sides were wrong. The first Mongol landing parties were met by samurai from the immediate area. The samurai attacked, deciding they did not need to wait for the army that had been dispatched by their government in Kamakura. They were surprised to discover that the Mongols used sophisticated battle manoeuvres and had crossbows that outranged Japanese bows and catapults that fired explosives. The samurai were forced to fight with tremendous courage. Dusk broke before the battle had been concluded and both sides retreated. That night a violent storm blew up, sinking many of the Mongol ships and blowing the remainder out to sea. The Mongols temporarily called off their invasion attempt.

Subsequently the khan sent another ambassador, this time with an ultimatum to the Japanese government. He ordered the emperor of Japan to travel to Peking and pay homage to him or risk a full-scale war. The Japanese reply was to cut off the ambassador's head and return it in a box. Soon after this incident the Mongols became heavily involved in fighting in China and five years passed before the khan again turned his attention to Japan.

This time he ordered the Koreans to build 1000 ships to carry a Mongol army of 50,000 men. This armada was to be accompanied by another even larger fleet, which was to set sail from China. In the summer of 1281 troops landed from both fleets at many points along the north and west coasts of Japan. The Japanese were better prepared this time and fought the Mongols at sea and on land. Armies from all over Japan headed for the fighting areas. The emperor and the clergy urged the people to fight and to pray to the ancestral spirits to help them to victory. The whole country joined in the war effort. A continuous battle raged for fifty days and stalemate seemed to have been reached. Then, as during the previous invasion, the elements came to the rescue of the Japanese. The whole of Kyushu was rocked by violent storms of hurricane force. They lasted for two days and two nights. By the time calm ensued the entire Mongol fleet had been sunk or blown away. Warriors left ashore were easily hunted down and killed. The invasion had failed. The Japanese named the hurricane the Kamikaze, or Divine Wind. The story of the intervention of the Kamikaze became a powerful part of Japanese folklore. Certainly until the atomic bombs on Nagasaki and Hiroshima it contributed to the belief, held until then, that Japan was protected by the gods.

Terry enjoyed drinking in the 'soapland' district of Fukuoka and we went there together on a few occasions. Every large Japanese city has a 'soapland', an area of bars, massage parlours, night clubs, restaurants and striptease joints. They used to be called 'Turkoland', but the Turkish Embassy in Tokyo complained and the name was changed. The new name derives from the practice in Japanese massage parlours of soaping the customer all over while he lies on a rubber mattress. This is for a basic fee. For an extra payment the masseuse will then use her own body to work the soap into a lather. The cost continues to rise depending on the customer's requirements. The outsides of the massage parlours in Fukuoka were garishly illuminated with bright neon lighting, and tough-looking louts stood by the entrances trying to persuade passing punters to go in. However, apart from being very expensive they are harmless places that cater for company men, usually drunk, socializing after work.

Soapland was fun to walk around. I discovered that Japanese men are not sheepish about their enjoyment of what is on offer. There was none of the furtiveness found in Soho or Times Square.

The Yakuza (the Japanese Mafia) are involved in soapland business, but at what level I do not know. I did see a number of the large, completely inappropriate American Cadillacs favoured by top Yakuza men cruising around the soapland streets. Japanese import taxes raise the price of these monstrous cars to that of a Rolls-Royce in Britain. The point of owning one is purely symbolic, since in Japanese traffic they must be a liability. Something which has often puzzled me is the fact that, in a job where one would expect anonymity to be essential, criminals the world over like to look like other criminals.

The girls who work in soapland districts normally come from country areas or distant towns. They earn as much money as they can in four or five years and then return home. Family or friends need not know what they have been doing and there is no loss of face. They set up a business, find an eligible husband and often do well. Japanese newspapers occasionally carry stories revealing that a well-known company boss or politician is married to a soapland girl.

This practice and the licensing of particular soapland areas by the government are part of a long tradition in Japanese society. In the seventeenth and eighteenth centuries entertainment for townsmen and for visitors alike (and often the main reason for going to town) was the brothel and the theatre. In large towns and at post stations along main roads like the Tokaido red-light districts were established and licensed by the government. Girls in brothels were graded and priced according to their class, background and their skills in such arts as singing, dancing, the tea ceremony, music and dress. Those of the highest rank were entitled to reject a customer they did not like. All, however, were controlled by pimps and were virtual slaves.

Foreigners in Japan during this time took advantage of the situation although the Catholic missionaries campaigned against it. Francesco Carletti, a seventeenth-century Portuguese visitor to Japan, wrote the following:

As soon as ever these Portuguese arrive and disembark, the pimps who control this traffic in women call on them in the houses in which they are quartered for the time of their stay, and enquire whether they would like to purchase, or acquire in any other method they please, a girl, for the period of their sojourn, or to keep her for so many months, or for a night, or for a day, or for an hour, a contract being first made with these brokers, or an agreement entered into with the girl's relations, and the money paid down. And if they prefer it they will take them to the girl's house, in order that they may see her first, or else they will take them to see her on their own premises, which are usually situated in certain hamlets or villages outside the city. And many of these Portuguese, upon whose testimony I am relying, fall in with this custom as the fancy takes them, driving the best bargain they can for a few pence. And so it happens that they will get hold of a pretty little girl of fourteen or fifteen years of age, for three or four scudi, or a little more or less, according to the time for which they wish to have her at their disposal, with no other responsibility beyond that of sending her back home when done with. Nor does this practice in any way interfere with a girl's chance of marriage. Indeed, many of them would never get married, if they had not by this means acquired a dowry.

To sum up, the country is more plentifully supplied than any other with these sort of means of gratifying the passion for sexual indulgence, just as it abounds in every other sort of vice, in which it surpasses every other place in the world.

The girls themselves were sold into prostitution by their families to alleviate the desperate poverty common to many people at that time. In some early records it is claimed that the girls were in fact sometimes better off in prostitution than at home. Prostitutes were generally bought from poor townspeople, although occasionally a samurai who had fallen on hard times would sell his daughter to a pimp. This would be for a high price since a girl of good social standing was able to attract better-paying customers.

Attractive girls from such backgrounds were also recruited as potential geisha girls. They trained for many years in the required 'womanly' arts before starting work as professional hostesses and entertainers. Geishas lived their whole lives in the pleasure districts of large cities, the floating world. They were valued for the quality of their conversation, singing and music playing. They did, of course, become lovers with some of the men they entertained, but they were not obliged, like prostitutes, to have sex with their customers.

The owners of brothels had the right to beat or starve their girls but cruel behaviour was uncommon since the girls were their stock-in-trade and could not work if they were injured. The law on runaway prostitutes was ambivalent. They were not obliged to return but the owner of the brothel was not prevented from forcibly taking them back. Brothel keepers and the procurers of girls held a respectable place in society and led ordinary lives, often amassing much wealth and influence.

Since those times there have been changes in Japanese attitudes to prostitution. Nowadays visiting a prostitute is not freely condoned although there is much less stigma attached to doing so than in the West. Also paying for sex in Japan is very expensive. This has resulted in a wave of new package trips for businessmen offering golfing holidays in Manila and Bangkok. The golf clubs never leave the bags and business girls in Thailand and the Philippines earn lots of yen.

The fact that the men go abroad for sex is some measure of the changes, albeit slow, in Japanese society: men no longer have it absolutely all their own way. In a respectable Japanese newspaper I read that in Tokyo there are Adonis bars staffed by handsome waiters and barmen. They are visited by well-off women who hire the men for sex. There are also stories in the more lurid newspapers of housewives who work as part-time whores out of choice for the money and adventure. Even to report such a thing would have been unheard of until recently.

In the evenings at Terry's apartment I made a point of watching the weather forecasts on the television (which was very accurate) since during the cherry blossom season local television stations broadcast reports of the amount of blossom on the trees. Eighty per cent cover is the peak before the blossoms start to fall. This degree of cover lasts only two or three days and it is during this time that cherry blossom viewing parties are held. Each district has its own favourite viewing sites where people congregate as the blossom reaches full bloom. They take picnics, lots to drink, tape recorders for music, and mats to lay out under the cherry trees. Noisy drunken parties are held late into the night.

One evening the cherry blossom reports were good and the next day Terry and I travelled south to the provincial town of Kumamoto for the cherry blossom festivities. The grounds of the town's massive concrete reproduction castle are a famous viewing site. The castle is a surprisingly authentic copy of the original, which was built in the eleventh century but destroyed by the Satsuma clan from Kagoshima in 1877. We took an afternoon train and booked into a business hotel early in the evening. The room was small. It contained only two beds and a pay television set with the normal channels plus one showing soft-porn. In one corner of the room a prefabricated portakabin-type structure had been placed. It contained a Japanese tub and lavatory.

We left the hotel and walked along a wide indoor shopping parade that ran parallel to the main road in front of the castle. After one or two tentative inquiries we found a busy *sushi* bar and ordered *norimakisushi* (vinegared rice wrapped in toasted seaweed) with tuna, prawn and green nettle filling to take away. We sat down in the lobby of the shop waiting for the order and watched the comings and goings of the well-dressed crowds. To me it felt like Christmas. To accompany the *sushi* we bought a chilled 2-litre screw-top can of Japanese Sapporo beer and a bottle of *saké*.

Thus equipped with food and drink, we joined the throngs heading for the castle.

The floodlit road leading to the outer gates was lined with cherry trees in full bloom. Beneath each tree a family, club or company group had staked out an area marked by a blue plastic groundsheet. Wherever I went in Japan blue ground-sheets were used for cherry blossom viewing. Why blue was a puzzle to me since it clashed with the colour of the blossom.

The atmosphere was loud and cheerful. I had naively ex-pected the beauty of the blossom and the poignancy of the falling petals to be acknowledged in some way, but my illu-sions were quickly lost amongst the eating, drinking and sing-ing.

In the inner courtyard of the castle the cherry trees were illuminated. The blossom looked splendid with the light shin-ing through it. The ground under the trees was a patchwork of blue plastic covered in a debris of picnic food, cans, bottles of Suntory whisky, a popular Japanese brand, and huge, mainly empty, *saké* bottles.

A family party invited us to join them. We clapped along rather self-consciously as family members sang their party pieces into a microphone. Terry embarrassed me by telling them I could sing 'My Way'. I changed the subject and asked if I could try some of their food. One of their trays contained slices of deep-fried lotus root filled with mustard. This is a Kumamoto speciality. I tasted it. It was extraordinarily hot and made my eyes water.

To one side of the main party area a rubbish tip had been started. Alongside it an odd-looking, youngish Japanese woman had built herself a cardboard shelter, using material from the tip. She furnished it with empty *saké* bottles and discarded paper lanterns. Some of them were still illuminated by burned-down candles. As the partymakers departed they gave her their leftover food and drink. She was having a good time in her little home, eating, drinking and holding court to a number of young men. They gathered around fascinated at this display of Japanese eccentricity. Terry and I went over to talk. She asked him to kiss her on the cheek, which he did. She looked grubby and unappealing to me and I wondered what on earth he was doing. I left them. Terry joined me later and said she had taken a dislike to him and had then refused to talk to or look at him.

At nine o'clock 'Auld Lang Syne' was played over the castle's Tannoy system. The people in the inner courtyard started to get to their feet and dutifully clean up. Many of the men were drunk, the women less so but still merry. The groundsheets were carefully lifted up by the partymakers so that the debris on them collected in a well in the middle. It was then poured into plastic bags and deposited on the rubbish tip. Given the size of the field, the number of picnickers and the degree of inebriation, the site was left very clean.

The floodlights went out and we all filed out of the castle. Outside celebrations were still going on. I saw a number of men collapsed under trees asleep in the foetal position. Later they would be carried home by wives or colleagues. A slight wind had developed and the blossom was blowing off the trees in a thin trickle.

We went back to the hotel. Many people were on the streets. The atmosphere was good-natured and friendly. I saw a policeman walk past a man pissing into a pot plant outside a restaurant. The man was held upright by his friend who accurately directed his aim for him by pushing with varying pressure on his back. Japanese men, like French men, urinate in public places quite openly.

In the hotel room we watched a baseball match on the pay television and then switched over to the soft-porn channel. The showing of pubic hair and by association the genitals is not allowed on Japanese television or in magazines or films. Cartoonists and film-makers have become experts at being as explicit and as titillating as possible without actually showing the offending organs. One famous male comic character has his penis separated from his body. He carries it around in his pocket. It has no pubic hair and can thus be freely portrayed. The head of the penis has a mouth, ears and a nose. It has a life

41

of its own and pops up in the most unlikely places, usually embarrassing its owner.

The soft porn we watched always had the same format. There was a man and a woman. She was on her back. He did things to her, never vice versa. In response she made loud noises and arched her back a lot. He mainly rubbed her breasts or massaged her vagina behind her raised knee or over opaque panties. Occasionally mock cunnilingus took place. It was initially funny rather than sexy, and then it was boring.

Kumamoto is said to have been the original target of the atomic bomb the American airforce later dropped on Hiroshima. On the day of the flight Kumamoto was covered in cloud and the bombers passed it by. To commemorate this bitter–sweet event a peace pagoda, donated by the Indian government, has been erected on a hill overlooking the city. I climbed up a steep back road to the monument to pay my respects. At the entrance to the pagoda there was an image of the Buddha, right hand lifted to heaven and left hand pointing to the earth. The figure stood in a tray of perfumed oil on an altar decorated with flower blossoms. I copied other worshippers and poured oil over the image with a wooden ladle, then closed my eyes and said a short prayer for world peace. A man selling homemade ice cream rode his bicycle and cart into the pagoda grounds and I went to buy one.

On the way down to Kumamoto I took the main road and discovered that the area of the peace pagoda is a favourite location for love hotels. Peace and Love.

I passed a large school. The pupils were coming out. They looked at me curiously, surprised to see a *gaijin* in a residential part of town. I reached the school gates just as a group of teenage boys came running out. They stopped outside the gates and formed a circle around two boys who started to fight. I was shocked at the viciousness of the bigger of the two boys. He punched and kicked hard and threw karate-style elbow strikes when the smaller boy tried to grapple him around the waist. I ran over and roared, 'Stop it!' They both did instantly, paralysed by my unlikely appearance out of the blue and the unexpected words shouted in a foreign language. Neither of them had the wherewithal to say anything. The bigger boy smiled and shrugged his shoulders as if to say the fight was nothing. The other had the expression of a kicked dog. I stood and waited, feeling slightly selfconscious, until the group split up and the bully went off with his friends.

Kumamoto is the home of Suizenji Park, which is one of the most attractive landscaped gardens in Japan. Before going back to Fukuoka, Terry and I caught a tram there and joined the family groups on a Sunday outing. Sunday is generally the only day when Japanese fathers spend time with their children.

Suizenji was constructed in 1632 as part of the villa grounds of the Hosokawa clan. It is designed as a miniature version of the old Tokaido highway. The park is remarkable for the way generations of gardeners have created from a natural habitat a completely artificial landscape. Each pruned tree, hill, patch of water or stone has been designed or chosen to represent a natural feature along the Tokaido.

As you enter the park a tiny Mount Fuji rising out of a grassy knoll comes into sight. Courting couples and old ladies in kimonos having their photos taken blocked the view all the time I was there. The path around the gardens starts at a miniaturized version of the original Nihonbashi bridge in Tokyo. It goes over a pond in which swim fat black and golden carp and continues past a tiny teahouse complete with thatched roof, raked pebble gardens and beautiful *shoji* (paper screen doors), and then around the mini Mount Fuji. Here I stopped to watch a party of Japanese pensioners ballroom dancing on a closely cropped lawn. They had a portable tape recorder and tapes of Joe Loss and his orchestra. It was an odd sight.

The path finished at a Shinto shrine reached through a pathway lined by fences of brightly painted red poles. At the shrine I pulled on the thick straw bellrope to attract the ancestral spirits that inhabited the place. I made my offering to them and left.

Zen Retreat

Great as is the value of Zen Buddhism for understanding the religious transformation process, its use among Western people is very problematical. The mental education necessary for Zen is lacking in the West. Who among us would place such implicit trust in a superior master and his incomprehensible ways? This respect for the greater human personality is found only in the East. Could any of us boast that he believes in the possibility of a boundlessly paradoxical transformation in experience, to the extent, moreover, of sacrificing many years of his life to the wearisome pursuit of such a goal? And, finally, who would dare to take upon himself the authority for such an unorthodox transformation experience – except a man who was little to be trusted, one who, maybe for pathological reasons, has too much to say for himself? Just such a person would have no cause to complain of any lack of following among us. But let a 'Master' set us a hard task, which requires more than inert parrot-talk, and the European begins to have doubts. For the steep path of self-development is to him as mournful and gloomy as the path to hell.

C. G. Jung*

While in Okinawa I had written to a Zen monastery located in an area near the foothills of Mount Fuji and very near my proposed route to Tokyo. I knew little about the monastery, except that it was Rinzai Zen and that in the past Westerners had stayed there. I inquired whether I might stay as a lay visitor or even perhaps attend a *sesshin*, a week of particularly long and rigorous Zen meditation. They are held at Zen monasteries once each month during April to August and October to February. *Sesshin* are demanding physically, emotionally and spiritually.

To my pleasure and surprise a reply was awaiting me when I

*Foreword 'Psychology and Religion: West and East', *Collected Works*, vol. II.

arrived in Fukuoka. It was from a woman named Joan, a resident member of the monastery. She said the head monk had given me permission to attend the April *sesshin*. It would be best if I arrived early in the afternoon of the first day, since the Japanese lay people attending normally got there in the late afternoon. It was a case of first come first served for places in the *zendo* (meditation hall) and dormitory. The letter also contained an underlined request not to quote Joan on any information she had given me. I thought this slightly odd.

The night before the *sesshin* was due to start I stayed at a small guesthouse in the mountain town of Shuzenji, on the Izu peninsula. All the other guests were Japanese OAPs. They were either shy or stiff with me. The noise of slurping and sucking at breakfast was exceptionally loud, but not as I thought because of the age of the diners. One of the breakfast dishes was a bowl of sticky beans that left threads of syrup between mouth and bowl. This syrup, I discovered, had the adhesive qualities of superglue. To get a portion of beans inside one's mouth required deft work with the chopsticks and a lot of sucking power. Hence the noise. I got into an embarrassing mess with mine and had to leave them. One old chap solved the problem by stirring into his beams the raw egg meant for his *miso* soup. This converted the syrup into a non-sticky, bright yellow, viscous liquid. I did not follow his example. In all my time in Japan I never got used to raw egg for breakfast.

I went to catch the bus to the monastery. The man at the ticket office told me to catch bus number 3, rather than go to bus stop 3. I waited for an hour and watched many buses go by, none of them a number 3. I went back to the office, complained and got my money back. I caught a taxi. From the window I saw a line of Zen monks coming into town. They wore black and grey robes over white long johns, large upside down bowl-shaped straw hats and rope sandals, laced up around their ankles and calves. They were from the monastery I was going to and later that day I saw them return, tired and dusty after their alms collecting.

The taxi driver left me at the foot of a large hill on the outskirts of town. There was no sign of a monastery, only a small gateway which opened onto a stone stairway. I put on my rucksack and climbed the steps. They led to a wide path that skirted a wooded area on one side and an old, heavily pruned plum orchard on the other. Ahead of me I could see the monastery buildings atop another hill. Around me there was evidence of construction work and tree felling. The monastery was more of a living, working community than were some of the polished and manicured tourist temples of Kyoto.

I walked up a steep flight of moss-mottled stone steps to the entranceway leading to the main temple buildings and living quarters of the monastery. Sitting in the sun outside the kitchens were a number of young monks. They were wearing loose trousers and vests and eating noodles. I asked for Joan, and she appeared from the shadows of the kitchen. She was slim, slightly worn-looking, not unattractive and, I guessed, about thirty-five. She was in fact fifty. She told me in low tones that she had been instructed not to speak to me; the head monk feared she might scare me away. She then quickly whispered that the monks did not like Westerners and that they bullied her. I wondered whether this was true or perhaps a reflection of Joan's own problems. Sometimes in Zen training initial respect for the Roshi (Zen master) and too much zealousness for Zen can later lead to disillusionment and mild paranoia. Also Zen in Japan is still very much a man's world and the path of Zen, already arduous and difficult, is even harder for women.

The monk in charge of guests interrupted our conversation and asked me in good English to follow him. He took me to the guest sleeping quarters and issued me with a *futon*, two blankets and a pillow. He then took me through the shoe routine. Wooden clogs for the toilet area, plastic sandals for the toilet closets, straw sandals for the wooden walkways around the *zendo* and sutra-chanting hall, and worn straw rope sandals for general use. The latter were difficult for me to put on since I could not wiggle the thongs between my toes without bending down and holding them apart. Later this caused me considerable problems.

I asked the guestmaster about the timetable, meditation procedure and other rules. He said I would be given all this information at the evening orientation session. He knew, however, that I spoke very little Japanese and that the monk giving the instructions spoke no English. He said they had no sutra books in *romanji*.

Zen training, especially during *sesshin*, requires that all personal and group activities are executed in a fixed and carefully delineated manner. This has the double effect of focusing the concentration of the students and of investing ordinary tasks with more importance than they are usually given. Thus for me not to be given details of the form, procedure and timetable of the *sesshin* I knew would prove a serious handicap to good practice.

It is fair to mention here that after leaving Japan I discovered that the monastery I am talking about is noted for its severe and traditional discipline. Visitors were not recommended to go unless they spoke fluent Japanese. I also discovered that other Western visitors had left in less than a day.

Before leaving the guestmaster showed me the room for *dokusan* (a private interview with the Roshi) and told me how many bows to make before entering and leaving the Roshi's presence. He said *dokusan* was an opportunity for confrontation with the Roshi. The monk was most serious but I began to imagine myself sitting opposite the Roshi, looking into his eyes and committing some outrageous Zen act to illustrate my enlightenment. Perhaps I could eat his vase of flowers. Joan told me the Roshi was powerful in *dokusan*.

I had an hour to myself before the *sesshin* officially started. From then on there would be no talking, reading or writing for seven days. I decided to collect my notebook and go and lie discreetly in the sun in the plum orchard. On the way Joan suddenly appeared and we had a furtive conversation.

She was most upset they had forbidden her to speak to me. She said it was wrong that I had no timetable and that there were in fact sutra books in *romanji*. Joan had been at the monastery for over five years and then she had left because of a vendetta with the new head monk. Now she had come back and said she intended to leave only on her own terms. To me she seemed most unhappy to be there and I could not understand what she had to prove or her motives for staying. She was also upset because that morning she had been told that she and I had to now attend the Roshi's daily *dharma* (discourse on a sutra or Zen story) talk. In the past Westerners had been allowed to listen to a taped English translation of one of the talks. This change of policy meant an hour's extra formal sitting in a timetable already containing ten hours' *za-zen* and it would make the start of the *sesshin* more difficult. To understand her disappointment it must be understood that a week's intensive *za-zen* is, at least for the first two or three days of a *sesshin*, extremely testing of one's stamina and capacity for pain. Experienced practitioners make sure they use any free time available for relaxation and to massage sore joints and muscles. Thus to lose an hour a day becomes quite important. Fortunately things do improve and after the opening few days one's mind and body start to settle down, the pain becomes unimportant, and the benefits of *za-zen* can really be experienced.

Joan asked me what posture I sat in during *za-zen*. I told her I used the Burmese position. She told me, quite rightly as it turned out, that the guestmaster would want me to sit in the half-lotus position. She recommended that I tell him my knees were damaged due to long sitting in previous *sesshin* and that the Burmese was all I could manage. For this advice I was most grateful. Joan was obviously a good person with kind intentions. However, the dichotomy she created for the monks was understandable. She was helping me but undermining their authority. I was thankful to her, but also uncertain that it was good for a newcomer like myself to be privy to the things she was telling me.

Our conversation was interrupted by a young boy about eight or nine years old. His name was Toshio. He had been sent by his father to the monastery for being naughty at school. It seemed an inept and inappropriate punishment to me. Toshio was lively and quick-witted. We took a liking to each other and he joined me sunbathing.

Lying in the sun, I realized how facing the prospect of seven days' loss of freedom, albeit voluntarily, was already focusing my mind wonderfully. The previous weeks of travelling freely about Japan had only that morning felt like a chore; now they felt like Paradise lost.

At 5 p.m. I went back to the *zendo* and met the seven Japanese lay visitors. They were all men, mainly middle-aged. They looked even more nervous, apprehensive and vulnerable than I felt. They were obviously in awe of the guestmaster and listened respectfully, even subserviently, to what they were told. They did not strike me as business executives, but some Japanese companies are now sending top employees for Zen training to toughen them up physically and mentally. The guestmaster told me in English that baths would be on the second, fourth and sixth nights and that on the fourth and seventh evenings noodles would be served instead of rice. For some reason this meant that on those nights we would have an extra twenty minutes' free time after the meal. This would be the only time I would have to run up the hill behind the monastery and look at Mount Fuji.

We all went together to the orientation talk. As expected, I could not understand any of it except for the visually clear instructions on how to unpack, use and wrap up the eating bowls we were issued with. During the talk we had to sit in the formal *seiza* position (sitting on your knees with your bottom resting on your upturned heels). This is quite normal for the Japanese and the traditional position for seated women, but it is difficult for Westerners. After an hour my feet had died and standing up was a struggle.

We went back to the *zendo* and took our places on our meditation cushions (*zabuton*). On each had been placed a small wooden name plaque in *kanji*. The *zendo* was divided into an inner and outer square of raised wooden platforms inset with *tatami* matting. The *zabuton* were placed on these. I sat in the inner square and formed part of a line of eight junior and experienced lay visitors. We faced on the opposite platform an equal number of senior monks. In the outer square facing inwards sat three of the lay visitors and Toshio. Joan sat in a corner of the outer square, facing the wall because she was a woman! Unfortunately Zen monasteries in Japan, with some exceptions, are still rooted in the past in their attitude to women.

The atmosphere, despite Joan's situation, was conducive to good sitting and I sat comfortably and with reasonable concentration for about an hour. I then started to wonder when the *jiki jutsu* (the timekeeper) would bang the gong for the end of the period. Normal procedure from my own experience was that each meditation period was divided into three thirty to forty minute sittings separated by five to ten minute periods of *kinhin* (Zen walking). *Kinhin* gives time for the blood to flow to one's sore knees and bottom and eases the pain of long sitting. Well, we just sat and sat. I could see the three men and Toshio in the outer square fidgeting uncontrollably on their cushions. Even one of the senior monks opposite me started to slump after what must have been an hour and a half of continuous *za-zen*.

Finally the gong went and to my surprise everyone immediately jumped up. They reached for their drinking cups, stored with our bowls on a shelf above each sitting position and then quickly returned to their cushions. I had no idea what was going on but speedily followed suit. From the right-hand entrance of the *zendo* two monks appeared carrying aloft large metal teapots. They came to each of us in turn, bowed swiftly, poured tea into the outstretched cups, bowed again and moved on. A wooden clapper was struck – the signal for all to sip their tea, which everyone did very fast. The two monks returned with the teapots. They completed a fast revolution of the *zendo*, holding the pots aloft but not offering the tea, and then went out again at the double. We put our cups away and returned to *za-zen*. I felt bewildered. Why go to the trouble of making and serving tea if the enjoyment of it was negated by deliberate haste?

By now the evening light had faded and the *zendo* was almost dark. The monks opposite me sat motionless and I settled into what I thought must be the last sitting before bedtime. Suddenly the gong went again. In a flash everyone had climbed off their cushions, put on their sandals and were already filing out of the *zendo*. I fumbled in the dark with my sandals, trying to get the thongs between my toes, irritated and in a panic. By the time I got them on the *zendo* was empty and silent. I rushed or rather shuffle-jogged in the direction everyone had gone and caught up with them just as they were all swapping sandals to go to the *hondo* (temple for sutra reading). I managed to creep into the dark, incense-rich hall just as the Roshi was making his entrance. He was a small, squat man with an impressive presence and the wrinkled face and large ears of an aged, wise elephant.

We sat in lines in the *seiza* position. Chanting started. It was slow and accompanied by the beat of a wooden drum with a deep tone. It was played at the pace of a dead march. The atmosphere was intense and serious. I would have liked to join in the chanting both to share in the service and to forget the pain in my legs. I wished I had a sutra sheet. I sat and attempted to generate some empathy for the people around me. All I experienced was alienation and the feeling that I had rudely gatecrashed into someone else's party. The chanting unexpectedly stopped. A tray of bean-jam sweets was ceremoniously handed around to mark the first night of the *sesshin*. I thought this at least showed some measure of compassion and pleasure in the joys of life. The interlude passed quickly, however, and the chanting, drumming and severe pain in my legs continued for another hour. Then it was finished.

I stumbled to my feet, just able to stand, and we walked back in procession to the *zendo*. I sneaked a look at my watch. It was 9.15 p.m. We sat on our cushions again and a monk banged the *han*, a thick wooden board, to begin the chanting of the closing sutra. After this and again at the double we filed out of the *zendo* and straight to the washing area. By 9.25 we had washed, been

51

to the toilet, unrolled and made our beds, undressed and got into them, and the lights had been put out. The timetable of the *sesshin* left only the absolute minimum of time for attention to personal matters. I guessed it was designed to confront the needs of the individual ego head on.

At 3.30 a.m. a gong went, the lights came on and the people around me who obviously knew the timetable leaped out of bed. They dressed, rolled up their beds and ran to the washing area. I tried to keep up with them but taken by surprise by the rush I lagged behind. They were already queuing for the toilets by the time I started to wash. I was about to clean my teeth when Toshio stopped me. Teeth cleaning was only allowed at night. By 3.40 a.m. everyone except myself was in the *zendo* and on their cushions. The unexpected speed of the morning start had made me nervous. I stood at the WC paralysed and unable to pee. By the time I got to the *zendo* the head monk was entering from the opposite side. I went to go in, but a monk roared at me to stop. The head monk took his place and then I was signalled to take mine.

Early morning meditation is the best for me. I particularly enjoy the stillness of this time and the gradual appearance of daybreak. I settled on my cushion and watched the uneasiness I was beginning to feel about this *sesshin* wash over me.

After an indeterminate period the gong went. This time it was the signal for morning service and everyone rushed off again to the *hondo*. As with the night before, I was left behind, held back by the time it took me to get my sandals on. During the service the *jiki jutsu* filed between our lines carrying a *keisaku*. This is a wooden stick used during meditation to strike a practitioner across the shoulders. It is normally used only at the practitioner's request, to help him refocus concentration and to relieve tight neck and shoulder muscles. The *jiki jutsu* was a big man with a thick neck. He used the *keisaku* freely. None of the monks seemed to resent this treatment, but I would have been angry if he had hit me uninvited. Later he pushed over with some force a monk kneeling next to him, I was not sure what for. I read later that it is this type of behaviour that Western visitors to Japanese monasteries find most difficult to accept and I was no exception. Actually observing this physical violence directly was a lesson for me. In the past I had been sure that Zen stories of extreme asceticism and violent behaviour were more mythical and symbolic than factual. Now I am not sure, and even as I write this several months later, I feel disquiet about this aspect of Zen.

We went back to the *zendo* and continued the morning meditation. I decided then to leave the *sesshin* after the morning work period. In the past I had considered leaving a *sesshin* before the end but had never done so. I had always been pleased I had seen it through. This was different. This *sesshin* felt too strongly like it was in the wrong place and the wrong time for me. My Zen daydreams of the previous day, which now seemed light years away, had turned sour. My subjective judgement, with its Western values, was that the monks participating in *sesshin* lacked compassion and dignity. The *sesshin* itself lacked direction. The Roshi was conspicuous by his absence. Contributing to these feelings was certainly my own sense of disorientation and alienation, created by the lack of basic information on what was expected of me and by the view of the guestmaster that I did not need to have it. Perhaps he judged it was the penalty I had to pay for wanting to take part in a quintessential Japanese experience without speaking Japanese. After all, he spoke English.

The morning meditation continued uninterrupted except for the serving of a little hot plum juice. Like the tea of the previous evening, it was served and drunk rapidly. There was no time to linger over its delicious smell or taste. I realized that my senses, even in the short time I had been sitting, were already heightened. A week in such an atmosphere following such a strict regime would have tuned me up to an unexperienced pitch, possibly opened me up sufficiently to experience a new level of reality. But despite this awareness I felt glad and right about my decision to leave. I did not doubt its wisdom for a moment.

Joan, bless her soul, passed me a note as we left the *zendo* for breakfast. I did not get a chance to read it until I had left the monastery grounds. It was a detailed timetable!

Breakfast was good but again served and eaten so quickly that there was no time to enjoy it. The monks serving the food moved swiftly from person to person. They continued to fill your bowl until you gave the signal to stop. One poor fellow forgot to give the signal and his bowl was filled to the brim. He then had to cram the food down his mouth to finish at the same time as the *jiki jutsu*, who oversaw the proceedings like a medieval king. He set the pace for the speed of serving and eating and bellowed commands as required. They served a sweetish rice gruel, sweet potato pieces, broccoli cooked with *miso*, pickled *daikon* and salted plums. All cooked to perfection and piping hot. Second helpings were available but nobody helped themselves to any for fear of not keeping up with the *jiki jutsu*. He was already washing and wrapping his bowl as the seconds appeared. Towards the end of the meal the serving monks entered again carrying the leftover food. Half bowing they ran from person to person, showing each the food, and then dashed out. Perhaps this procedure was to show nature is plentiful, but I'm not sure.

I told the guestmaster I was leaving. He was genuinely surprised and said, 'But it's only just started!' I told him I had made a mistake, I respected what they were doing, but it was wrong for me. We went to see the head monk. He looked like a twenty-year-old despite being nearer fifty. He did not look like the bully Joan had claimed he was but I was unable to judge either way. They talked to one another in Japanese and then suggested to me that I should see the Roshi. I told them I would not do that, that it would be rude to meet him and then leave. They laughed like two boys. The atmosphere softened. The guestmaster unexpectedly told me to come back again if I wanted to.

While I was packing my rucksack Joan came over and said she would like to see me before I left. She had a very small Japanese house at the edge of the monastery grounds. She rented it from the monastery. They preferred her to live there rather than in the main area of the monastery complex. She gave me directions to the house and at her request we walked there separately. Joan was worried that I had left because of her, or that the head monk would think I had. I assured her that neither concern had any foundation. According to Joan, the Roshi had been very good several years ago. She had given up her career and house in London to study with him. Now she said he was ambitious and more devoted to buildings than people. He had recently been ill and spent a lot of time in hospital. His influence at the monastery had waned. Another problem according to Joan was that nowadays Zen monks were not monks in the traditional sense. They were the equivalent of parish priests. They stayed at the monastery for two to three years and then went home to take over their family parish. Joan was honest and frank. She said Zen had broken her spirit. She was slanderous about any Zen teacher – including my own – and any other group I mentioned, and was obviously poisoned by her own experience of Zen in

Japan. Nevertheless I respected her honesty and felt concerned about her welfare. We said goodbye. I left and she went back to the *sesshin*.

The sun was shining and on the road outside the monastery I jumped up and down shouting, 'I'm free!'

Six months later and back in England, my interest in Zen is undimmed despite my experience in Japan. In retrospect I see that the time I spent at the monastery was valuable, but I now believe that the future of Zen lies as much with Western teachers and students as it does with those from Japan. Zen practice in Japan is often too rooted in traditional attitudes and it is in danger of fossilizing.

If a person particularly wants to study Zen in Japan I would recommend that he or she initially join a Zen group at home under the auspices of a recognized Zen teacher of genuine lineage, and gain as much experience as possible before going. Choose the monastery you wish to visit carefully and write well in advance to ask permission to stay. A very good book devoted to the subject of Zen training in Japan has recently been published. It is called *Zen Guide* and is written by Martin Roth and John Stevens,* and I would recommend it to anybody planning such a trip. Meanwhile, remember the Sufi story of the young man who left home and spent the rest of his life searchng for the Tree of Knowledge. He never found it and many years later returned home, old and tired. He went into his back garden and there growing in the centre was the Tree of Knowledge.

*Wetherhill, New York, 1985.

History Lesson

They also have rites and ceremonies so different from those of all the other nations that it seems they deliberately try to be unlike any other people. The things which they do in this respect are beyond imagining and it may truly be said that Japan is a world the reverse of Europe; everything is so different and opposite that they are like us in practically nothing. So great is the difference in their food, clothing, honours, ceremonies, language, management of the household, in their way of negotiating, sitting, building, curing the wounded and sick, teaching and bringing up children, and in everything else, that it can neither be described nor understood.

Now all this would not be surprising if they were like so many barbarians, but what astonishes me is that they behave as very prudent and cultured people in all these matters. To see how everything is the reverse of Europe, despite the fact that their ceremonies and customs are so cultured and founded on reason, causes no little surprise to anyone who understands such things. What is even more astonishing is that they are so different from us, and even contrary to us, as regards the senses and natural things; this is something which I would not dare to affirm if I had not had so much experience among them. Thus their taste is so different from ours that they generally despise and dislike the things that we find most pleasing; on the other hand we cannot stand the things which they like.

Alessandro Valignano, sj*

The above account comes from an anthology of writings by European explorers of Japan in the sixteenth century. Despite the influence of Western culture on modern Japan, much of what is written in it still holds true today. This is perhaps because, until the end of the Second World War, mainland

*Michael Cooper (ed.), *They Came to Japan: An Anthology of European Reports on Japan, 1543–1640*, Thames & Hudson, 1965.

56

Japan had never been invaded successfully by a foreign power and Japanese culture developed in an atmosphere of isolation. Japanese history has thus had a profound influence on the contemporary customs, beliefs and manners of the Japanese people, and to understand them some knowledge of their history is essential.

The first inhabitants of Japan are believed to have been a Caucasoid race who called themselves Ainu. They were bigger than the ancestors of the present-day Japanese, lighter-skinned, and the men were much hairier. Ainu women were said to have been very beautiful. Even today women of Ainu descent are in demand in Japan as models. The Japanese people are descended from an Asian Mongoloid race. They migrated to the islands that are now Japan over 10,000 years ago. Gradually, over thousands of years, they overran the Ainu, who were pushed farther and farther north. Several thousand Ainu still survive. Most of them live in small isolated villages in Hokkaido, the northernmost main island of Japan.

Before about the fourth century AD Japan was a collection of independent states rather than a single nation. In time the various ruling families made alliances, one of them gradually gaining precedence over the others and winning paramount control over the whole country. From this background emerged the original imperial family. The history of the time is only vaguely known but all the lineal ancestors of the present emperor are believed to have descended from one family which flourished in the third century AD.

In Japanese mythology, however, the emperor is believed to be a direct descendant of the sun goddess Amaterasu. As such he is a divine being who has the power to intercede with heaven on behalf of mankind. Oddly, except in the earliest times, this has never meant that the emperor has automatically ruled the land. In fact throughout Japanese history the emperor, although spiritually venerated, has rarely had any political power. Instead, control of the country was divided amongst various clans. Overall power at any particular time was held by the clan leader (*daimyo*) with the strongest army. Such a leader was later to become known as the Shogun. There was no fixed rule of succession when an emperor died, and any of his sons could be chosen to be his heir. To ensure an emperor of their own choice powerful *daimyo* would often assassinate unwanted successors to the title.

Between the seventh and ninth centuries Japan developed trade links with other nations and particularly China, but in the late tenth century she broke off all relations with the rest of the world and underwent two hundred years of isolation. It was during this time that the samurai developed as a distinct warrior class and the ethics of the *bushido* (the Way of the Warrior) evolved. 'Samurai' literally means 'one who serves' and the samurai were soldiers who owed total allegiance to a particular *daimyo*. Samurai were themselves divided into three groups. At the top were those who served the Shogun, second were the samurai of ordinary *daimyo* and at the bottom were those who had lost their masters through war or politics. They were called *ronin*. They roamed the land; some worked as mercenaries, others turned to crime. *Ronin* and their exploits feature in many Japanese stories, films and plays.

From the twelfth until the sixteenth century, Japan was subject to almost continuous civil war. Battles were fought between opposing clans seeking overall power or by emperors trying to gain a political control that matched their spiritual rule of the land. The situation improved in the late sixteenth century when General Oda Nobunaga defeated the other most powerful *daimyo* in the country, General Imagawa, to become ruler of virtually all Japan. Nobunaga was both a ruthless soldier and a devotee of the arts. Under his guidance there was a renaissance of interest in poetry, theatre, dancing and fashion, which all flourished in the relative peace of his reign. He also encouraged trade with the outside world and European arts and Christianity became fashionable. He was less generous at home and declared war on a number of Buddhist sects which he believed were divisive and warmongering influences. He ordered the complete destruction of a complex of monasteries on Mount Hiei, a religious centre near Kyoto, and the death of all the monks, mainly by burning. Nobunaga in his turn was murdered by one of his own generals. The killing took place in a temple where Nobunaga was performing in a Noh play and was in retaliation for an assumed insult.

Toyotami Hideyoshi succeeded to power in 1582. He had a different outlook from Nobunaga and thought that foreign influences were weakening the spirit of the Japanese nation. He slowly introduced laws aimed at reducing the influx of foreign goods and people, and at the same time reinforced traditional feudal patterns of society.

Hideyoshi gradually subdued all the remaining outposts of independent *daimyo* and by 1590 was the ruler of a united Japan. Through the changes he instituted in the government of the nation Japan gradually became more insular and rigidly feudal. One outcome of this was the increasing persecution of minorities, particularly Christians.

Hideyoshi died in 1598 and was succeeded by Tokugawa Ieyasu, who moved his headquarters from Kyoto to Edo (now Tokyo). From here the Tokugawa family dominated Japanese life for the next 250 years. One after another the Tokugawa shoguns maintained a hostility to all foreign religions and secular influences and carried out a policy of national seclusion. Japanese were prohibited from travelling outside the country and foreigners were not allowed in. The laws that were enacted during the Tokugawa era (1603–1868) help to explain many contemporary Japanese attitudes.

The intention of the Tokugawa shoguns was to control every aspect of Japanese life in every corner of the land. The place a person lived, what he ate, the type of clothes he wore, even the posture he adopted and the way he slept were dictated by the state. A succession of Tokugawa shoguns tightened up the already rigid Japanese class system and used the division of the people into classes as a method for maintaining and perpetuating their own power. The arts continued to flourish, however, and life was relatively peaceful and secure for common folk as long as the rules were obeyed and there was enough to eat. Once in power, the Tokugawa clan began their ordering of the class system from the top. The emperor and his court were restricted to Kyoto. Their duties were confined to the purely ceremonial. The Tokugawa family maintained the emperor in his position but only to confer the title of Shogun (full title, Commander-in-Chief for Quelling the Barbarians) on whomever the family nominated. The emperor's upkeep and that of his courtiers were maintained by grants of land from which they kept the income. This maintained them in a respectable rather than a luxurious life style. The emperor's activities were supervised by government officials and were limited to cultural pursuits. Although he was only a figurehead, the emperor's title was hereditary and the line of succession was sustained. This was of potential danger to the Tokugawa regime and it later led to their downfall.

Like the emperor's, the affairs of military lords were closely monitored by the Shogun. They were controlled by the allotment or dispossession of the territories from which they were entitled to collect taxes. The rights to land were given only in exchange for oaths of allegiance The number of armed men they had, the types of fortifications around their castles and even their social contacts were controlled. Government inspectors ensured that they upheld their agreements, and if they broke any they were punished by loss of land or exile to a distant part of the country. As an extra safety measure the Tokugawa shoguns maintained control of the three largest cities – Edo, Kyoto and Osaka – and gave the lands around them to close relatives or loyal allies. The final weapon in the Shogun's armoury for ensuring control of clan lords was the Law of Alternate Attendance (see p. 96). Under this law nobles were required to maintain a residence in Edo and some members of their family had to live there permanently. They could be used as hostages in the event of any trouble. The lords themselves had to reside in Edo for one year out of every two. The upkeep of two homes, together with all the travelling between them in suitable style, plus a legally required involvement in public works and duties, ensured that the nobles were kept busy and short of money.

After the emperor and noble lords, the Buddhist and Shinto clergy were the group most likely to make trouble for the Shogun. They were thus split up under the Tokugawa regime into individual sects which were themselves divided into separate independent units. No cooperation or joint decisions were allowed between groups and rivalry for land and income was encouraged – a perfect example of divide and rule.

The rest of society was split into four groups. In descending order of status they were samurai, farmers, craftsmen and merchants. Women belonged to the same class as their fathers or husbands. Membership of a particular class was hereditary. The samurai did not work as such and they considered the pursuit of money dishonourable. They were supported by taxes from the farming class, who suffered considerable hardship maintaining the top-heavy warrior class. The samurai enjoyed many privileges and during the Tokugawa years had little to do since there were few battles to fight. They were, however, expected to set a good example to the rest of society and to lead sober and honest lives. In this time of peace the samurai brought the arts of fighting to a high point of skill, ceremonial and ritual, although expertise in real battle fighting and war tactics diminished.

Farmers, the main bulk of the population, were the next on

the social ladder. Although not at the bottom of the social order they were the most exploited of the classes. Upon them depended the rice harvest and thus the samurais' and in turn the Shogun's food and prosperity. They had to work hard and were not allowed to leave the vicinity of their birthplace. On top of these hardships most also suffered poverty.

Craftsmen had less status than the farmers but they were probably happier. They had more mobility and freedom in the way they led their lives. Master craftsmen, particularly swordmakers, were valued for their skills and lived in the security of a particular lord's protection.

Merchants were at the bottom of the social ladder since they did not produce anything and worse than that, they were motivated by profit and dealt with money. In spite of their lowly position in the social order, the merchant class later became the main beneficiaries of the Tokugawa era and as a group they were largely responsible for later changes in cultural and social attitudes.

The Tokugawa system of government began to break down by the late eighteenth century. The samurai had been emasculated by lack of opportunity to do battle. They had become as interested in the arts of the tea ceremony and calligraphy as in that of sword fighting and had lost their authoritarian grip on the country. Both they and the peasants had grown very poor and the newly prosperous merchant class had emerged as a force for change. Because of their influence Western explorers and traders had been allowed to enter Japan again. In 1867 the young Emperor Meiji ended the long cloistered existence of the imperial family by putting himself forward as the country's leader. He became the focal point for a Japanese nation that had lost its cohesion. After fighting off Tokugawa loyalists he attained full power in 1868 and began his revolutionary reign, the Meiji Restoration.

Emperor Meiji for the first time formally instigated Shinto as the official state religion. Since the Shinto belief is that the emperor is of divine lineage and a living god, this new ruling gave him total power over the nation. He used it primarily to abolish the old class system and to institute new laws and reforms that were intended to give more human rights to all Japanese. From this beginning Emperor Meiji led Japan over the next forty years from being an isolated, agriculturally based, feudal society to a powerful nation with a modern navy and army, good railways, a parliament and an industrial base. The changes he wrought were not without their excesses, however, since the Japanese seem to be unable to make gradual changes. Things Japanese were despised for a period and many historical buildings and relics were destroyed. At the same time American and European cultures were admired. During this period there was even a cult for marrying Western women in order to improve the nation's bloodstock. During the Meiji era Japan won the Sino-Japanese war in 1895–98 and defeated the Russians in the Japanese–Russian war of 1904–5.

Meiji was succeeded by his son Yoshito in 1912. He was renamed Emperor Taisho. Not much is known about Taisho since he suffered from mental illness and was kept out of the public eye. The illness is said to have been caused by lead poisoning; apparently this came from his wetnurse who had used white lead to whiten her breasts, a common practice of the day. His condition made little actual difference to the way the country was governed since ministers sympathetic to the spirit of the Meiji era continued to be in charge. Japan entered the 1914–18 war on the side of the Allies and emerged as a modern military nation with worldwide prestige. The Showa era (1926–   ), ruled over by Emperor Hirohito, Taisho's son, saw the next radical changes in Japanese history.

By the beginning of the 1930s Japan's industrial economy needed overseas markets and new sources of raw materials. At the same time there was an upsurge of nationalism and a growing sense that Japan was the natural leader of mainland Asia and the Pacific basin. Both factors led Japan to invade Manchuria in 1931, followed by a full-scale invasion of China in 1937. They withdrew from the League of Nations and at home totalitarian politics and militarism grew in popularity. The movement was unlike the fascism of Italy and Germany since the emperor remained the secular and spiritual head of the state around whom a consensus form of government was centred. The Japanese were, however, to join forces with Hitler, and on 7 December 1941, with the bombing of Pearl Harbor, they entered the Second World War.

Japan's subsequent military defeat was followed by the Allied occupation. A ruined economy and the devastation of most of its major cities forced Japan into another period of rapid change. The Japanese were economically and spiritually broken by their first military defeat in history and by the horrific way in which the war was finally ended with the atomic destruction of two major cities. A new start was required and a re-examination of national values was undertaken at every level. This process is still going on today. Western industrial nations are themselves now having to face the same need for national reappraisal. It is, however, less urgent, and thus slower and less effective than Japan's has been.

Japan's desire for expansion is now concentrated on industry and international trade, and her success in these areas is matched by an increase in the standard of living, high employment and improving social welfare at home. Alongside this achievement there are also small but not yet significant signs that nationalism, militarism and cultural chauvinism are again growing trends. At the moment they are manifested mainly in calls for a Japanese army with an offensive as well as a defensive role and in the growth in the number of religiously based political parties of the right wing, such as Soka Gakkai.

After the war the Japanese parliamentary system was revised to become a constitutional democracy. The prime minister is elected from the ruling party in the National Diet. The constitution forbids the use or development of nuclear arms and the formation of an army for reasons other than defence. It expressly denies the emperor any political power. He is defined as the symbol of the state and derives his position only from the will of the people. Civil liberties as wide-ranging (or as narrow, depending on your view) as those in Britain are written into the constitution. The voting age is twenty.

Because of their history the Japanese people have developed certain unique qualities that perhaps explain their economic success in the last forty years. They manage to encompass simultaneously a sense of mutual responsibility and competitiveness, and honesty and loyalty. These attributes are combined with an unquestioned acceptance of long working hours and an enthusiastic commitment to job and employer. On top of this, they have developed a keen understanding of the needs of specific home and overseas markets and the ability to fulfil them.

Their success started in Western markets where the Japanese originally captured the imagination of the working classes with their consumer goods. For instance, they produced cheap, reliable cars with lots of extras that became standard. The motoring press despised these cars but they sold in large quantities. The

Japanese gained in confidence and their approach became more sophisticated. They began to make cars that pleased both the driver and the family man. Nowadays Japanese cars have universal appeal. The design of specific models is tailored to suit local needs and they can be seen everywhere from the market-places of impoverished Third World nations to the freeways of America. By good marketing, an eye and ear for what people want, the application of the latest technology and the ability to produce good-quality goods quickly and cheaply, the Japanese now dominate world markets.

On top of this the Japanese government have protected their own market from foreign competitors by imposing rigorous import quotas and duties. International pressure is changing this, but the problem for the Japanese government is that the Japanese prefer to buy Japanese. They are used to buying goods which have been carefully researched to fill a particular market need. Foreign companies often fail to do this properly and prefer to buy and sell goods which have been successful elsewhere. For this reason it is often only the foreign novelty goods which have no direct application that sell well.

The Japanese have moved a long way since Commodore Perry and his black ships opened Japan to the outside world. In those days the Western nations had enormous influence on Japan, now it is very much a two-way process. There are even some indications that in the future Japan will become the most dominant force, more influential than the USA, in shaping Western economies and attitudes.

Fukuoka to Kyoto

I left Fukuoka to travel to Kyoto. In order to see more of rural Japan I decided to take the slow train along the relatively undeveloped north coast of Honshu rather than the direct *shinkansen* express along the more built-up south coast. My first stop was at Shimonuseki, a small town just inside Honshu, across the Kanmon Strait from Kyushu. Here I was to change trains to join the San-In line. Before catching my connection I left the station to buy a *bento* lunch for the journey. *Bento* are beautifully packed takeaway meals. They can be bought from shops and stalls in and around railway stations all over Japan. Each area has its own speciality. *Bento* lunches are one of the treats of a train journey in Japan.

The basement of the department store adjacent to the station was a cornucopia of food. Many of the counters displayed free samples of what they were selling. This is standard practice. It offers a simple and free way for tourists to taste a selection of some of the enormous variety of uniquely Japanese foods. The *bento* counter had a hundred or more dishes to select from, plus many boxed assortments. The choice for me was simple; triangular patties of *sushi* rice, each with a separate sheet of very thin, crisp *nori* seaweed. The *nori* is wrapped around the *sushi* just before it is to be eaten. Sold in this way, the seaweed wrapper stays crisp. Sold already wrapped, it gets soggy.

I left Shimonuseki on a three-carriage limited express train for Masuda, a town known for its hot springs. The train followed the coastline for over 200 miles. We passed seaside fishing villages and travel-brochure lookalike sandy beaches under clear blue skies; inland, bamboo groves, orange orchards and rice paddies cut into steep wooded hillsides. The journey was a pleasure.

During this train ride I started to realize that, except in the flat

plains areas, of which there are few, Japan is not densely populated. Even outside the extensive mountain regions the Japanese countryside is exceptionally hilly. Habitation is restricted to flat patches of land between the hills which are just too steep to build on or, often, even to terrace for cultivation. There are few moors or fells as in Britain. The land is either flat or rises sharply. Japanese country walks require climbing boots rather than wellingtons.

Several times during the journey a young man selling food and drink from a trolley came up and down the train. He bowed when he entered the carriage and bowed again when he left. He did this even when I was the only passenger. On one occasion I feigned sleep when he appeared, but he still bowed. I wondered if he bowed to empty carriages. On one of his patrols I bought tea from him. It came in a small, square-sided plastic bottle with a screw-top lid that doubled as a cup. In the bottle I could see a tiny green-tea teabag. The tea was very fresh and hot.

The Japanese are even more particular about their tea than the English are. Different grades of tea are blended at different temperatures. Boiling water is never used. Ordinary green tea is made with water at about 90° C. To achieve this temperature boiling water is cooled by pouring it into an empty teapot; the water from the pot is then poured into the teacups and back into the pot. Now the tea is added, allowed to brew and poured. It remains hot because the cups and pot have been preheated. The best Japanese tea is extremely expensive. It is made from the first young shoots at the top of the tea bush. They are hand-clipped. The second-best tea is made from hand-cut secondary shoots. For ordinary-grade tea the bush is trimmed by machine.

At one point in the journey the train stopped for a time at the station of a small fishing port. From the window I could see several squid boats in the harbour. They were easily recognized by the large lightbulbs strung out above their decks. The Japanese love squid. In Tokyo and the larger towns there are restaurants and shops that specialize exclusively in squid dishes. A popular street snack is squid baked in small balls of dough. Squid boats sail out to sea only at night. At sea they switch on their lights. On a clear night they can be seen from the land as bright specks in the darkness. The squid are attracted by the light and swim to the ship. The fishermen throw out lines fitted with hooks and then drag them in. The squid get caught up on the hooks. No bait is needed.

After five hours the train reached Masuda and I got off and went to the small information office adjacent to the station. The young attendant could speak no English but, once she had got over her shyness and I had used my Japanese vocabulary in all the limited combinations possible with twenty words, she managed to help me. I wanted to find a local hot-spring, Japanese-style inn (an *onsen* in Japanese), situated by the sea. Japan is a volcanic country and consequently there are numerous hot-spring areas. Hot-spring baths are popular for their curative properties as well as for just relaxing in with family or friends. *Onsen* are built near or over a hot spring. Guests stay at them not only to enjoy the waters but for the food for which they often have a good reputation.

There were many *onsen* in the vicinity of Masuda. I picked one called Araisokan, which was a thirty-minute ride by local bus from Masuda. I had made a lucky guess: the inn was perfectly situated. It was built on a small cove facing the Japan Sea. Adjacent to it was a fishing village set on a round curve of sandy beach, deserted except for odd pieces of fishing equipment.

The girl at the tourist office had rung ahead and I was expected. This is a good idea. In out-of-the-way places a *gaijin* appearing out of the blue can flummox the proprietor, so much so that she might say she had no vacancies. This, she believes, saves face for both parties. Without advance warning she would assume that a place so Japanese could not be what you really wanted.

I left my shoes at the entrance, put on the hotel slippers and followed the maid to my room. It was ten-*tatami* size and over-looked the sea. At high tide the water reached the sand beneath the sliding window. The maid made tea for me and left. I drank the tea, sitting on the *tatami* floor and looking out to sea. The sliding paper screens and windows had already been pulled back.

After relaxing, I changed into the kimono-style dressing gown provided and left my room to find the hot-spring room. It was large, steamy and noisy with the sound of running water. The west wall was glass and faced the sea. The spring was directed from its underground source to flow from a miniature volcanic rockface artificially constructed to overhang the big bath. I soaped and rinsed myself at one of the low taps plumbed into the wall opposite the bath and then got in. The water was very hot but comfortable to lie in if I did not move. The floor of the bath had a thin coating of some type of volcanic material carried

69

along by the spring. It swirled around as I got in and then settled. I soaked and watched the sun setting behind clouds out to sea. Two Japanese men joined me. Later in the evening I saw them on the beach with their young girlfriends. The four of them were wearing their dressing gowns. They took flashlight photographs of one another. The girls giggled a lot. I decided they were having an illicit weekend. The men did not treat the women as wives and were too old to be bachelors in Japan.

I went back to my room just in time to answer the phone call telling me dinner was on its way. I sat with my legs folded under the low table and waited. The maid arrived carrying a very large black lacquer tray. She put the tray down just inside the door, bowed to me, picked the tray up again and carried it to the table. On it were hand-made pottery bowls, delicately painted porcelain plates and a variety of lacquered dishes. Each of them contained food. I sat like a king as she put the meal out. She backed away from the table, bowed again and left.

The food looked exquisite, a work of art. I was torn between just appreciating it and getting out my camera to photograph it. One of the problems I have with collecting material for a book is that in the process of recording an event I fail to experience it fully. In physics they call it Heisenberg's Uncertainty Law.

Some of the dishes were unknown to me and others so well disguised that I did not recognize them until I tasted them. There were three raw, very fresh shrimps in a tiny hand-woven straw basket, and whole sea bream dipped in thin batter and deep-fried in extremely hot oil. All of it, bones as well, was edible. The fish was garnished with a fan of finely sculpted bamboo shoots. *Sashimi* of squid, tuna and bonito garnished with fresh chrysanthemum leaves and grated *daikon*; forest mushrooms; mountain potatoes; seaweed in vinegar garnished with fresh herbs; vegetables delicately cut into flower shapes and a gently fried fillet of sole with pickled ginger were the other dishes I recognized. There was also a clear soup with a cluster of very small white fish floating in it. I did not eat them. They looked albino, as though from an underground lake not reached by the light. For dessert there were slices of fresh pineapple garnished with two perfectly shaped strawberries.

Two maids came to clear away the table. Afterwards they laid out the *futon* mattress and made the bed. I watched on the television the Giants, Japan's top baseball team, play the Carps from Hiroshima, then went for a walk along the dark beach. On the way back to the hotel I almost garrotted myself on a gut fishing line strung out between two bamboo poles stuck into the sand, ten feet apart.

The next morning before breakfast I ran several laps around the beach. The local fishermen were not sure what to make of me. Hairy legs and joggers are a rare sight in that part of Japan. The fishing village was old and quite primitive. As I ran back and forth an old lady collected buckets of sea water and carried them back to her small house. It faced directly onto the beach. I assumed she had no running supply of fresh water.

Breakfast at the inn was the Japanese equivalent of a full English breakfast. *Miso* soup with beancurd, pickled *daikon*, a piece of smoked fish, rice with toasted *nori* seaweed to crumble over it, and a raw egg to stir into the soup. I would have preferred toast and coffee.

After breakfast I joined the other guests for an obligatory morning soak in the spring-water bath. I then collected my things and went to pay the bill. The proprietor was a middle-aged woman. She sat next to a paraffin stove behind a desk near the entrance. There was a large metal teapot on the stove. She offered me a cup of tea. We talked for some time, she in Japanese and I in English. Neither of us understood the other but she did not seem to mind. Before I left we had our photographs taken together on her camera.

From Masuda it was a short train journey down the Yaaguchi line to Tsuwano, a Japanese mountain village. I had wanted to visit Tsuwano since reading about it in a JAL in-flight magazine. The author had been eulogistic. He described Tsuwano as, 'locked away in a mountain valley . . . the single most romantic hideaway I've seen to date.' He had found it by chance. On the day he arrived he was even lucky enough to see a centuries-old samurai horseback archery competition which was held just once a year. He stayed in a fantastic *ryokan* (a traditional Japanese inn) with a wonderful garden and a maid so beautiful that she would have stopped the traffic in Tokyo. It was also cheap! There were carp in the village drainage ditches.

Well, I discovered that Tsuwano is a lovely village but I had to strip away the romantic expectations engendered by the article before I realized it. It is not 'locked away' but is a popular tourist spot dubbed 'little Kyoto' in the guidebooks. The archery competition is famous and it would be hard not to know it was taking place. The carp in the ditches are fat and beautiful; they are looked after as a tourist attraction by the village council. The lady proprietor of the *ryokan* said her prices were much higher than those quoted in the article. She was fed up with phone calls from prospective visitors. The maid was too embarrassed to show herself.

Tsuwano is in fact, in travel brochure language, a well-preserved traditional Japanese village set in a mountain valley. There are good mountain walks in the area, well-maintained and interesting temples and shrines, and a variety of designated cycle routes. They are chosen and marked out by the village tourist office. The office provides village and cycle maps in English and the addresses of numerous *minshuku* (Japanese family homes that take guests) for accommodation. Cycles were available for hire at a number of places. On some days in April and May there is even a steam locomotive service to Tsuwano from Ogori, a stop on the *shinkansen* line.

I enjoyed Tsuwano but only stayed one day. The morning after I arrived it was overrun by coachloads of Japanese old-age pensioners. This day must have been the start of a pensioners' holiday season. From then onwards I was to meet OAP groups anywhere that was remotely on the tourist routes. They travelled in coaches in parties of a hundred or more. Like groups of old people (and children) anywhere, they were preoccupied with themselves and not very sensitive to other visitors or the places they were visiting. Two pensioner couples had the room next to mine in the *minshuku*. They were up early and by 6 a.m. had their television set on. It was loud. The men were drinking *saké*. I was both irritated and amused. I pulled back the screen door of their room and admonished them in English. They looked at me blankly and then turned their television set off. They continued to drink, smoke and talk loudly and did so through breakfast as well. Delinquents.

I left Tsuwano on a Sunday to travel to Kyoto. Train services were reduced and the journey was going to take over twelve hours. It is not a good idea for a tourist to arrive in a Japanese town after early evening. The tourist information offices are shut and *minshuku* expect their guests to arrive for dinner. Alternative accommodation is normally expensive. To avoid this problem I decided to stop before Kyoto at Yonago, a town on the Sanin coast about eight hours by rail from Tsuwano. The journey was uneventful. I did, however, see some interesting sights out of the window. Women working alongside men on building sites and railway gangs. Many old people in their Sunday kimonos who had badly bent backs, the result of years of working in rice fields. Mothers carrying babies on their backs and wearing extra large coats that covered them both, with the baby's head sticking out through a special opening. Children in school uniform and crash helmets riding their bicycles in orderly single file.

At Yonago the ticket collector wrote down for me the address of a business hotel. I found it after the usual difficulty of locating anywhere in a Japanese city. Even locals find it confusing because of the complexity of the Japanese address system. The only single room vacant in the hotel was claustrophobically small. I did not take it, and there was nowhere else at a price I was willing to pay. I decided to rush back to the station and catch the connection to Kyoto. The train was almost empty. The only other passengers in my carriage were three well-dressed businessmen. They were half drunk and, after a period of desultory conversation with one another, they curled up on their seats and went to sleep. I sat with my feet on the seat opposite and looked out into the darkness. At one station I had time to buy a takeaway bowl of hot noodle soup with floating pieces of vegetable *tempura*. Delicious and cheap.

The train arrived at Kyoto station at 10.30 p.m. The man at the reception desk of the first hotel I went into spoke English. He told me there was no hotel vacancy in the city. This particular day was the busiest of the year in Kyoto. It was the first day of a three-day national holiday and the start of the cherry blossom viewing season. I went back to the station intending to sit out the night in the waiting room, but the station entrance had been closed. I began to look around for a bench to sleep on, imagining to myself the story of the birth of Jesus if Mary and Joseph had arrived in Kyoto at the height of the cherry blossom season. I then remembered an old travellers' haunt I had stayed at in Kyoto ten years previously. It was called Tani House. Tani-San was a relaxed Japanese woman who provided cheap dormitory accommodation in two rooms in her home, which was on the outskirts of the city. I rooted her number out of my bag and rang. She said she was full but that I could sleep that night on the floor of the family living room. I caught a taxi and asked the driver to ring Tani-San for directions on how to get there. I stayed at Tani House for a week and would recommend it to any budget traveller. Address and details are given on p. 184.

73

Kyoto

Kyoto is the religious capital of Japan and, until the end of the Edo period in 1868, the home for many centuries of the imperial family. It is a lovely city of temples, gardens and shrines, as well as fashionable shops and restaurants. The gods of spirit and mammon live happily cheek by jowl in Kyoto. The atmosphere of the city was captured for me in the Gion district. Here there is a famous centre where the classical Japanese arts are performed, and next door to it is a very busy betting shop, itself adjacent to the entrance of Kennin-ji Temple. While I was there cherry blossom was blowing down the streets, which were busy with traffic, geisha girls, monks and tourists. Once inside the grounds of Kennin-ji there are quiet places to be found and, like other contradictions in Japan, silence and noise exist side by side.

Kyoto is a magnet for tourists, both Japanese and foreigners, but there is so much to see and do that crowds only form at the most popular places. Avoid the city on public holidays and avoid the best-known temples at weekends. Otherwise it is easy to get around on foot, by bus, subway, hired bike or, if you are in a rush, by taxi. There are probably more guidebooks on Kyoto than on any other city in the world. One of the most beautiful Zen gardens in Kyoto, and possibly the least visited, is that of the Koto-In Zen Temple, a small sub-temple of Daitoku-ji with only three buildings and a garden. It is very near Tani House, where I was staying. Koto-In was established in 1601 by a famous military leader, Hosokawa Tadooki. Despite having a wife who was a follower of the outlawed Catholic faith, he was a leading general in the army of Toyotomi Hideyoshi, who, as we have seen, later became Shogun. For his loyalty Hosokawa was rewarded with large demesnes of land. However, he devoted himself to the study of Zen and also became one of the most

distinguished pupils of the famous tea master Sen Rikyu. Lord Hosokawa and his wife, Lady Gratia, are buried in the gardens of Koto-In Temple.

I arrived at Koto-In at 9 a.m. just as the doors were being opened. I was the only person there apart from the old door-keeper. The altar room in the main temple was dark and I could not easily distinguish the buddhas and other images that surrounded the altar itself. The temple rooms were divided by *shoji* paper screens which could be opened or closed to make rooms of different sizes or be taken away altogether to make one large room. There was a tangible atmosphere of peace and calm as I passed over the *tatami* floors onto the verandah overlooking the gardens. Outside, the bright sunlight struck eye-catching angles off the bamboo fences, *shoji*, roof eaves and unpolished wooden beams of the monks' quarters. Whatever I looked at had an air of dignified, elegant simplicity; even the doorkeeper, now sweeping leaves off the moss-covered lawn, had it in the way he moved his body and brush.

I was left to wander wherever I wished. At first I was too excited to sit and enjoy the peace; instead I decided to take some photographs. This was difficult. Unzenlike, I wanted to capture everything. I exposed a whole reel of film and was then able to relax. I sat down on some steps overlooking a bamboo grove.

My legs were dappled with sunlight shining through the new leaves of the maple trees in front of the grove. The maples must be beautiful in the autumn when the leaves turn golden red. I heard Zen clappers somewhere in the grounds of Daitoku-ji calling the monks to meditation, prayer or maybe morning tea.

My reverie lasted for a while until it was disturbed by the arrival of a bridal party who were using the temple gardens as a backdrop for their wedding photographs. They seemed embarrassed by my presence, so I left and went for a late breakfast. I spent the rest of the day at the launderette and the *sento*.

Sento are public washing baths. In the past Japanese town house usually did not have baths, and *sento* were invented as a public service. They provide hot running water for washing and a large bath full of extremely hot water for soaking in. Many also have mineral baths, whirlpools, electric baths and cold plunges. *Sento* are found in most cities and small towns. They come in a variety of shapes and forms, ranging from Gothic exaggeration to Zen simplicity. Until recently their popularity was declining but in the last few years they have become fashionable again, especially with young people, and, like old cinemas, they are being renovated in their original style.

If you are an independent tourist, travelling in Japan and staying in budget accommodation, *sento* are excellent places in which to relax at the end of the day. They can be identified by their tall, narrow metal chimneys and the distinctive flame logo painted over the entrance.

Nowadays *sento* are not mixed, although both the men's and the women's baths are usually looked after by an old lady *obesan*. She sits on a platform inside the entrance to the baths astride the wall that divides the two sides. Men go in the right-hand entrance and women in the left. As you enter you pay the *obesan* and buy from her, if you need them, shampoo, soap and razor. Towels can be hired but most Japanese make do with a small piece of cotton towelling called a *tenugui*. This is used initially as a flannel and then as a towel for drying off. *Tenugui* are practical for the traveller since they are small and light and dry quickly.

The accepted procedure in a *sento*, if you ever have the good fortune to visit one, is as follows. Put your clothes in one of the lockers and lock it with the numbered wooden key provided, which you then keep on your wrist. Inside the bath area you will notice, plumbed into the walls about 12 inches off the ground, a series of pairs of hot and cold taps. Sit at one of these on one of the low plastic stools provided. Pour water over yourself with one of the small bowls scattered about the bath floor. Now rub soap into your flannel or *tenugui* and soap yourself all over. Rinse the soap off thoroughly and then very gingerly sit in the hot tub. Add cold water if it is unbearably hot. Soak for a while. This will open up your pores. Get out of the bath and repeat the soaping and rinsing procedure to get really clean. Shampoo and shave if you wish. Now sit in the hot tub again, or in one of the other types of bath, and relax. Before you leave the bath area rinse yourself with cold water or sit in the cold plunge.

In the changing room you will probably see an armchair fitted with massage rollers. To use one you need to put the correct coins into the slot in the arm of the chair and adjust yourself against the moving rollers. They can be moved up and down your back with a control lever near your right hand.

That evening at Tani House I met two Japanese men in their twenties. Both had worked in America for a short time and spoke some English. They expressed surprise that in the eyes of the rest of the world Japan was a success story. They said it did not feel that way to them. They still looked upon America as the land of opportunity and riches. This feeling is quite common in Japan. For some reason the Japanese see themselves as a Third World nation. They are bewildered, and think it is some kind of deception when the West complains about their protectionist policies and demands they accept the responsibilities of a leading nation in the world. The young men I spoke to supported Prime Minister Nakasone and his strong stand against the Russians. They admired Mrs Thatcher. Both were unemployed because they did not want to become company men. They were nevertheless nationalistic.

We talked about Yukio Mishima, the famous Japanese novelist who committed ritual suicide, and they became upset when I suggested he had been a homosexual. They claimed he was not and that there were very few homosexuals in Japan. This is not true. I pointed out to them that I had been surprised to discover that even amongst samurai warriors homosexuality had not been unusual. This was too much for them to stomach and the conversation ended in stony silence.

In fact amongst the samurai class of the seventeenth century and later homosexuality was quite normal and not considered sinful. Priests of various Buddhist sects taught that homosexuality

77

was natural and even virtuous compared with sex with women. These teachings were, as one might expect, mainly from the sects that forbade sexual relations with women. Their rationale was that commiting sodomy with a boy did not cause him discredit or his relatives any dishonour because he had no virginity to lose, and in any case sodomy was not a sin. The priests, despite their questionable motives, had considerable influence. Their views helped to form a school of thought among upper-class samurai warriors that homosexuality was a purer, more idealized, form of love than the heterosexual variety. In fact the Tokugawa government banned male prostitution, but this was not for moral reasons: rather they were worried about samurai mixing with and being influenced by low-class male prostitutes. During the Tokugawa era the government took strong measures against any trend that threatened class boundaries or the status quo. For instance, they banned men and women appearing together on the stage, which gave rise to the important tradition of transvestism in Japanese theatre.

This sexual ambivalence is exemplified by Kabuki theatre, in which all the women's parts are played by men, and such all-girl reviews as Takarazuka Young Girls' Opera Company, in which all the male parts are played by beautiful young women. Apart from providing an arena for covert homosexuality, the transvestism in Japanese theatre gives the Japanese, as actors or audience, room to vent the frustrations created by a society in which the public role-playing of men and women is rigidly divided. The actors and actresses in their role changes do not attempt to impersonate a particular man or woman but rather to present an idealized version of universal man or woman. To play their roles well they must study and practise intensely in their daily lives the characteristics of the opposite sex. Then they reproduce the impression of man or woman, rather as an artist, intimately familiar with his sitter, might paint a portrait. Yoshi-sawa Ayame, an early and great Kabuki artist, said that the ideal woman could only be expressed by an actor. He called it 'the synthetic ideal'. This admiration of the synthetic is encountered frequently in Japan. I think this is because they are able to judge the artificial and plastic substitute as a thing in its own right rather than as a copy of something 'real'. For this reason, although transvestite clubs and performers are popular all over Japan, they never have the camp overtones of their Western equivalents.

*

The following morning I planned to visit the Silver Pavilion Temple and the famous Zen rock garden at Ryoan-ji Temple.

The Silver Pavilion was built in 1488 by the Shogun Ashikaga Yoshimasa. The main plans for the temple were inspired by the design of the Golden Temple built by Yoshimasa's grandfather, Shogun Ashikaga Yoshimitsu. However, the Silver Pavilion is perhaps the more interesting of the two because Yoshimasu was an aesthete who had a special interest in the arts, and he included in the temple buildings rooms designed especially for pastimes such as flower viewing, moon watching, the tea ceremony, incense smelling and poetry composition.

Much to my disappointment, when I got to the temple it was closed to visitors because of a dispute between the temple authorities and the city administrators. I decided to visit the Golden Temple instead. Its correct name is Kinkaku-ji Temple but both the second and third floors of the main building are plated with gold, hence its popular name. The gardens are particularly lovely. They contain a pond called Kyoko-chi, or Mirror Pond, in which the Golden Temple is reflected.

On the day I arrived the pond reflected only a large white parcel. This was the temple wrapped in a billowing voluminous white cloth while undergoing repairs. I was annoyed that I had not been warned of the situation before paying the entrance fee. This had probably been overlooked in the confusion, as the dispute that had closed the Silver Pavilion was also causing problems at the Golden Temple. The city authorities wanted to impose a tax on temple entrance charges. The temple leaders insisted they needed all the money for maintenance and running costs, whereas the city claimed that much of the money was in fact used to support monks and temples outside Kyoto. The outcome of the dispute was that many smaller temples had closed their doors to visitors. Others, like the Golden Temple, had devised a system of payment whereby outside the temple visitors were given an empty envelope in which they placed a donation towards the support of the temple. This was handed in at the entrance and the visitor was then allowed in free. The new system did not change anything but allowed both sides to keep face.

I enjoyed the temple grounds with their evergreen trees, isolated rocks and dark, moss-carpeted lawns, which give the carefully planned look of untutored nature so prized by

Japanese gardeners. Unfortunately it started to rain heavily so I left to get some lunch. I found a busy noodle shop in a back street and ordered a bowl of green noodles in soup. They came in a very large green ceramic bowl, topped with chopped leeks and fried *tofu*. An egg had also been stirred into the soup. The phone kept going with outside orders. Every now and again the chef popped out with a wooden shoebox-shaped container holding steaming bowls of noodles. Outside he had an autobike with a carrier on the back. It was suspended from springs in such a way that the shoebox when loaded onto the carrier remained level, even when the bike went around corners.

I walked south from the Golden Temple following the base of Mount Kinugasayama (really a steep hill, not a mountain), which separates it from Ryoan-ji Temple, the home of the Zen rock garden. I found a path that runs over the mountain into the grounds of Ryoan-ji. The path, which is worth searching for, is little used and shown only on large-scale city maps. It was steep and overgrown, but at the top I had a splendid view of Kyoto.

There are three basic types of Japanese garden: the tea garden is usually designed by tea masters as a site for the tea ceremony; the hill garden, designed for private estates, is a small park with miniature artificial hills; and the flat garden. The Zen garden at Ryoan-ji is an extreme version of the flat garden. In this style few trees or shrubs are used and the most common elements are stones, sand and gravel. They are designed, like a painting, for contemplation. Several of the best Zen gardeners were also well-known painters in ink. In this medium they intended, with just a few strokes of black ink on white paper, to evoke an atmospheric natural scene. Their gardens were three-dimensional evocations of this idea and they used sand or gravel instead of silk, and shrubs, trees or stones instead of brush strokes. The garden at Ryoan-ji was created by Soami, a famous ink-line artist. It consists of only raked gravel and five stones and certainly obeys the injunction written by an anonymous sixteenth-century painter and gardener: 'Caution should be taken not to be too anxious to overcrowd the scenery to make it more interesting. Such an effect often results in a loss of dignity and a feeling of vulgarity.'

I sat and looked at the garden for over an hour. I was in a restless mood, however, and my enjoyment was more to do with the novelty of the surroundings and the antics of some of the Japanese visitors than a tranquillity induced by the garden.

Perhaps with the garden to oneself and many days to contemplate it a more profound understanding would develop.

The entrance ticket to the temple and gardens includes a leaflet with a description of the garden. I quote it here to show that, even at a famous Zen temple, conceptualism, the enemy of Zen, is present.

The Zen Garden of Ryoan-ji Temple

Let us sit down quietly and contemplate this garden of sands and stones.

Soami, the famous artist who created this garden, here expressed his understanding of Zen enlightenment with great simplicity, requiring neither words nor precepts to convey his limitless message.

We can view the garden as a group of mountainous islands in a great ocean, or as mountain tops rising above a sea of clouds. We can see it as a picture framed by the ancient mud wall, now in itself regarded as a national treasure, or we can forget the frame as we sense the truth of this sea stretching out boundlessly.

Soami's eloquence will appeal for ever to those who will look at the garden with inner eyes. Absorbed in this scene we, who think of ourselves as relative, are filled with serene wonder as we intuit Absolute Self, and our stained minds are purified.

In Zen, everything, even a leaf of grass, expresses ultimate Reality. Thus we can say that this simple garden of itself suggests to us absolute value.

This garden is such a profoundly meaningful one, beyond any comparison with others of the world, that it might better be called Mu-tei – 'Garden of Nothingness', or Ku-tei – 'Garden of Emptiness', than Seki-tei – 'Garden of Stones'.

Ryoan-ji,
Kyoto

To the northeast of Kyoto is the steep-sided Mount Hiei (850 m). Mount Hiei is mentioned frequently in Japanese Buddhist literature since for twelve centuries it has been the site of Enryaku-ji, at one time the most influential Buddhist monastery in Japan. Nowadays there is a cable car almost to the summit. From the top footpaths lead down to the temple complex. I decided to explore the mountain to flesh out my imagined picture of this home of so much spiritual endeavour.

I took the Keifuku electric railway, a private line, from Demachiyangi station in north Kyoto to Yasayuen station, the last on the line. The only other people in the train were a party of eight men and one woman. They were dressed in what I took to be their best casual clothes, but they were nevertheless still shabby. For Japanese they were uncharacteristically loud and coarse and reminded me of football supporters at home. They had picnic food and *saké* with them. The woman paid the conductor for all their fares.

At Yasayuen I followed a river around the foot of Mount Hiei until I arrived at the cable-car station. The car went up the mountain at a very acute angle. It was frightening enough to make two children on board squeal with excitement and fear. The area we stopped at near the summit was being turned into an artificial ski slope and it was messy with construction materials. I followed a wide path up to the summit. Here the site was being developed into an entertainment centre and Musak was blaring from a public address system. The views of Kyoto were magnificent, but any expectations I had of experiencing the spiritual nature of Mount Hiei at this point were lost to the sounds of 'Yesterday' floating over the mountaintop.

I took a path down from the summit which I thought would lead to the monastery ground. It did not and I got lost several times in a maze of footpaths before meeting with two French Zen students who were walking up the mountain. They had a detailed map of Enryaku-ji and its surroundings and they showed me the right direction to follow.

The monastery, a series of different temples each with its own deities and rituals, has a fascinating and chequered history. In the eighth century Emperor Kammu decided to build a new capital city to be called Heian-Kyo on the site of present-day Kyoto. Before the work started he ordered a Buddhist monk, Saicho, of the Tendai sect, to establish a temple on Mount Hiei to protect the new city from evil spirits. The temple became the centre of a monastery complex that grew in size and importance as rapidly as Heian-Kyo below. By the eleventh century Enryaku-ji contained over three thousand temple buildings and had become the headquarters of the Tendai sect. The monks had their own army and, far from protecting Heian-Kyo, they warred with any political or religious faction that opposed their control of the city and even with the incumbent emperor. Saicho, during the early years of the monastery, had 'discovered' Shinto gods on Mount Hiei. He claimed they were in fact ancient Buddhist deities and suggested that the emperor owed allegiance to them and thus to the spiritual leader of Enryaku-ji.

The monks of Mount Hiei continued to influence Japanese political and religious life until the sixteenth century and the arrival of General Oda Nobunga. He is quoted as saying: 'If I do not take them away now, this great trouble will be everlasting. Moreover, these priests violate their vows: they eat fish and stinking vegetables, keep concubines, and never unroll the sacred books. How can they be vigilant against evil, or maintain the right? Surround their dens and burn them, and suffer none within them to live.'*

In 1571 Nobunga invaded the mountain, burned every temple to the ground and executed every monk. The monastery was re-established in the seventeenth century but never regained its former power. It is still, however, the headquarters of one of the Tendai sects, and the number of temples it contains and the size of the grounds make it one of the largest monasteries in Japan.

The principal temple buildings are collected in two areas known as the eastern and western precincts. The eastern precinct is more easily reached by tourist coaches and when I arrived in the vicinity I met a lot of visitors on the paths that led between the tree-hidden temples. I decided to walk west towards Jodo-in, which houses Saicho's tomb, and was soon on my own among tall dark trees. Jodo-in is situated in a depression in the hillside and enveloped by trees. It is a still, quiet place. Saicho built the original temple, but the present three buildings date from the Edo period (1603–1867). Saicho's tomb is housed in a small shrine behind the main hall. In front of the stone fence which surrounds it there are many stone lanterns, small pagodas and a holder in which burns incense presented as an offering to Saicho's spirit. To the left of the tomb stands a linden tree. After enlightenment the Buddha gave his first teachings under such a tree. I sat under its branches to test it out.

I walked back into the woods. The air was cool. I found a place to sit down that was warmed by a beam of sunlight and ate the small picnic I had brought. Enryaku-ji is known for the severe spiritual practices of some of its monks. Sitting in that peaceful spot I could not imagine voluntarily undergoing the hardships they suffer. Traditionally they undertake three Austere Practices. For those involved a term of practice is 1000 days divided into ten units of 100 days each. Jodo-in is the temple for

*Gouverneur Mosher, *Kyoto: A Contemplative Guide*, Charles E. Tuttle, 1964.

the practice of Sweeping Hell. Here the monks rise very early and spend half the day brushing the temple grounds and the other half in prayer. At the Mudo-Ji-Dani (the Valley of the Still Temple) in the eastern precinct they rise at 2 a.m. and then set out to walk to each temple in the monastery complex, praying at each one on the way. No easy task with 125 temples. At Yokawa Temple in the small northern precinct monks undergoing the third of the Austere Practices are required to spend six hours of each day inside the temple buildings, chanting sutra and praying, for a continuous period of 1000 days.

I spent the rest of the afternoon on Mount Hiei wandering slowly from temple to temple, each of which has its own special story. I was fascinated by the spiritual life they represented but was nevertheless glad not to be a monk.

Late evening I walked back up to the summit of Mount Hiei and took the cable car down to catch the train back to Kyoto. The party I had arrived with were on the station. They were now the worse for drink. We boarded the train and the other passengers avoided them. I sat near them fascinated by the way the woman seemed to be organizing the outing. The smallest and most mischievous man in the group sat next to her, almost in her lap. Again, she paid all their fares. They got off the train on the outskirts of Kyoto. The other passengers watched their progress out of the station with keen interest.

Up to now I have only talked about Buddhist temples, but Shinto shrines are to be found in many places in Kyoto as well. *Jinja*, as they are called in Japanese, are much smaller and simpler in design than the Buddhist temples. They are constructed from unpainted wood and often have thatched roofs. In the countryside small, rudimentary *jinja* are found marking a particular field or a local beauty spot. The Japanese make offerings at a *jinja* either to their ancestors or to the guardian spirits of the particular shrine. This is a commonplace thing to do and city shrines are busy places with people going in and out all day. There is a water trough by the inner shrine and before making an offering the worshipper pours water over his hands and rinses his mouth. After this symbolic purification he attracts the gods by clapping his hands three times and pulling on a rope attached to a wooden clapper on the ceiling of the shrine. A silent prayer is then given and an offering of fruit, money, incense or *nusa* (small strips of white paper symbolizing purity, sold at the shrine entrance) is made. I enjoyed following the ritual myself.

The entrance to a *jinja* is easily identified by a *torii* gate, guarded on either side by a carved stone lion–dog. The mouth of one dog is open and the other is closed. They symbolize the sounds of 'Ah' of birth and 'Mm' of death. A visitor to the shrine passes between the dogs and is reminded that the line between life and death is a short one.

Shinto is a religion unique to Japan and, alongside the philosophy of Zen Buddhism, its beliefs have influenced Japanese history and the Japanese character. Known by the Japanese as Kami-No-Machi, the Way of the Gods, Shinto has its origins in the myths of the tribal people of ancient Japan. They believed that in all the world only their islands were populated and that they themselves were the children of the gods. Followers of Shinto worship the spirit god Kami, whose nature is manifested in all the things around them such as rivers, mountains, trees, rocks and animals. Each deity has a place in a hierarchy of power which culminates in the sun goddess Amaterasu. Amaterasu is worshipped at the imperial shrines of Ise on the Shima Peninsula on Honshu, where the spirits of all past emperors are enshrined. Lesser deities are the local *kami* who look after just one village or one family's fields.

There are no fixed scriptures in Shinto. Its rituals and ceremonies are directed at receiving a blessing from the gods for a particular function or event. They are a daily part of Japanese life. Shinto priests, wearing long flowing robes and tall lacquered silk hats in a style unchanged for a thousand years, are called upon to officiate at all manner of occasions. Ceremonies are held to bless babies, marriages, children starting school, new construction sites, even new cars. The priest carries a pine branch (*sakaki*) which he waves over the subject of the ceremony as a sign of purification and blessing.

Confucianism, brought to Japan by Chinese merchants in AD 400, had an important influence on Shinto beliefs. This is still evident in the traditions of contemporary Japanese society. Confucianism was a code of ethics which emphasized loyalty to the family, with the father as patriarchal head, as one of its most important rules. The first-born son directly succeeded his father. Mothers were to be respected and loved. Ancestors were to be revered and their memories respected. Loyalty was one of the highest virtues.

These ideas, coupled with Shinto teachings that the emporer was a living *kami* and that the spirits of the dead lived on, produced the patriarchal, ancestor-worshipping culture of traditional Japan. The emperor as a living god was given allegiance by the nation. He was the symbolic and literal father of the one family of the Japanese people. Such beliefs lived on until the Second World War, when the Japanese suicide squads sacrificed their lives for the emperor. This influence is still evident in the patriarchal attitude of Japanese companies towards their workforce and the loyalty to them of their employees.

Followers of Shinto do not see its beliefs or practices as an obstacle to following other religions. In some Japanese households I have seen a Shinto offering to the ancestors, a Buddhist statue and a Christian crucifix all collected together in one room for worship.

Shinto, with its emphasis on the basic purity of all things, was fertile ground for the assimilation of Buddhist and especially Zen Buddhist beliefs. The two schools of thought have never merged but the majority of Japanese subscribe to both. In fact many Buddhist temples either contain within their grounds, or are adjacent to, a Shinto shrine. The Japanese use rituals from one or the other to mark important events in their lives. For instance, marriage is usually a Shinto ceremony and burial a Buddhist one. In daily life the practice of followers of both Zen and Shinto is to be pure in heart and accepting of the changing nature of all things.

Salarymen and Japanese Impressions

Before I left Kyoto a Japanese teacher invited me to dinner to meet a group of salarymen whom he taught English. They wanted to practise English with an Englishman. We had a long conversation and I learned a lot about their working lives. This was most interesting since salarymen are the backbone of Japan's economy and their attitudes and work practices have played an important role in its success.

On the street of any Japanese city the man walking past you wearing a white shirt and a blue suit, and indistinguishable from the men around him dressed in the same way, is probably a company or salaryman. There are salarywomen, but they are fewer in number than the men. A salaryman benefits from lifelong employment with the same company. He joins the company between the ages of eighteen and twenty-two. The expectation on both sides is that he will remain with the same company until he retires. A person who leaves a company position is considered potentially unreliable. An unemployed ex-companyman over the age of thirty will find it very difficult to get a new position.

Employment conditions for a salaried position are detailed and known in advance. One of Terry's partners had trained as an osteopath. Her first interview for a job was at a Tokyo hospital. At the interview she was told her salary expectations up to the age of sixty, her pension details and even how much she might expect for her funeral expenses. She was eighteen years old at the time! The thought of her life being mapped out was so depressing that she turned the job down. She is now a self-employed businesswoman. For many other people, however, particularly men who plan to marry and have a family, the attractions of being a salaryman outweigh the disadvantages.

87

Apart from job security, the company provides health care, housing and leisure facilities and even arranges holidays. This system suits the average Japanese, who likes conformity and the safety of a social structure he or she is part of and understands.

The Japanese propensity for conformity and orderliness also helps to explain why ritual is so important in Japanese life and business. Ritual is an outward display of an inner belief in and acceptance of certain codes of behaviour. It vests importance in people, places and events, and adds a certain dignity and significance to everyday matters. Ritual gives conformity the breath of life. It has been lost in Western culture, replaced by a search for expression in external material objects. Fulfilling these needs has ironically been one of the sources of Japan's great economic success.

Salarymen work six days a week. They always work late. This is expected and essential if they are to get promotion. Sometimes they even waste time in the day to be sure they have something to work on late in the evening. After work they go out for a drink with other companymen. This is also expected. The tradition is catered for by the numerous bars and restaurants found in the business area of any large city. Large sums of money are spent in these areas. It is an important method of circulating money in the economy. A wife expects her husband home late. She might even worry that he is not getting on at work if he gets home early each evening.

Employees expect their bosses to trust them and to leave the responsibility of day-to-day matters solely in their hands. A boss who wanted to make decisions about mundane matters would lose their respect. Once a group of employees trust their managers their loyalty to them will be total. Good relationships between management and the people who work for them are normal in Japanese business. Both parties are usually on close terms and will go out drinking together. However, even outside work company status is recognized and deferred to.

Union officials are entitled to see the company's accounts and to know what profit they are making. Wages and wage rises are related to the profits. There is no parity system with others in the same profession who work for a different company. In the past, wage rises have been about 5 per cent higher than cost-of-living rises. A typical Japanese worker saves on average 30 per cent of his wage. Interest rates for borrowing are low.

Wages are calculated on the basis of an employee's expected

day-to-day domestic expenses. Added to this is a twice yearly bonus for holidays, a car, luxury items and any other expenses concomitant with a person's position in the company – membership of a golf club for upper management, for instance.

Strikes take place but they are normally only ritualized stoppages. Every year during the second week in April employees go on strike for one or two days to support their yearly wage claims. During this time they go into the company premises but do not work. They wear red armbands to signify they are on strike. On strike days they do not go drinking with management!

Salarymen always try to get to work. If there are no buses or trains because of snow or a strike they will walk. Three weeks a year holiday is the norm. They are taken in one- or at the most two-week stretches.

By comparing work practices and attitudes such as these with our own in Britain, it is easy to see why the Japanese are experiencing such economic prosperity compared to our own decline. There is, however, a price to pay. Salarymen work long hours, often under competitive and stressful conditions. Sunday is the only day they have time to spend with their wives and children. This puts marriages under strain. It prevents any real relationship developing between a father and his children and puts total responsibility for their upbringing onto the mother. As a group, salarymen are experiencing an increased level of cigarette consumption and lung cancer and a rising incidence of suicide.

In the Tokyo area commuter train journeys are sometimes two hours long. The crowded, smoke-filled train is a symbol of oppression for the unhappy salaryman commuter. Committing suicide in front of the train taken to work each day becomes a ritual act of freedom. This event occurs often enough in the Tokyo vicinity for there to be a special train and crew to deal with it. The train is fitted with a winch and the crew with aluminized head-to-toe boiler suits. They winch up the commuter train and remove the body. The track and train are then hosed down and the journey restarted. On board the train meanwhile the commuters are getting anxious, sucking in breath and considering how late for work they will be.

It should be added as a postscript that ritual suicide is rooted in Japanese culture. There is no social taboo against it as there is in the West. Also the Japanese government have not seriously campaigned against cigarette smoking. Social attitudes towards the habit are still much the same as they were in Britain and the USA twenty years ago.

After my discussion with the salarymen I concluded that we in Britain would certainly benefit from some of their practices but that I, for one, did not wish to emulate their life style. Given the stark choice of unemployment, poverty and uncertainty in the North of England, or a job, prosperity, stress and suffocating security in Japan, I am not sure which I would choose. Probably the former.

The conversation with the salarymen obliged me to articulate as a visitor my impressions of Japan. Later I wrote them down.

Like the French, the Japanese seem to find as much as they want within the borders of their own country. Their life style is uniquely Japanese despite the influence of American and European culture and contains within it the various social structures and opportunities needed for leading a full life. The people I met were honest and usually helpful and cheerful. I encountered little sense of distrust or distaste for foreigners. Women, despite my expectations, seem to take an equal role to men in the life of the country. Japan is expensive for the tourist but with an awareness of the cost of things and an understanding of how the system works, one's outlay can be contained. Public transport is reliable and efficient but unavoidably expensive. It rains a lot but in long bursts rather than in frequent showers. The weather forecasts on the television are very accurate. The countryside is beautiful with a variety of landscape. It is not crowded since much of it is too mountainous to be habitable. Industrial areas are polluted and depressing. Cities are busy, prosperous, well looked after and have many amenities. Private houses and apartments are small and, to my taste, claustrophobic.

Throughout my journey I found Japan a clean country. Even Tokyo was free of litter. In the large cities I visited I saw groups of street cleaners regularly collecting rubbish and sweeping the pavements. Both men and women did the job. They wore white gloves and designer overalls. Passengers on trains took their own rubbish home. Shinto emphasizes cleanliness and purification rites in its ceremonies and I wonder if this is the basis of Japanese fastidiousness over personal and public hygiene.

What I did not like about Japan was the noise and the rush. In Japan the sound of one hand clapping is drowned, usually by the canned, two-handed applause of television shows. Paradoxically, in the home of Zen people are nervous of silence. Almost without exception public places, department stores, restaurants and shops have piped music and/or television. Sometimes both are played simultaneously. I was told of a new-style Japanese coffee bar where they have individual booths, each fitted with headphones. You buy a coffee, select a tape of your choice and listen to it in private. I was attracted to the idea since it would provide the uncommon opportunity in Japan of sitting in silence. Once, while in a *sushi* bar, I observed a rare example of Japanese individual initiative. A customer actually asked the waitress to turn off the loud music. This she did, without question, at the double quick pace reserved for a customer's request. Blissful silence ensued but it lasted less than a minute. It was too much for the waitress to bear. She left the music off but switched on the television. Noise is essential to the Japanese. They do not like to feel alone.

To rush about is another Japanese characteristic. This is fine in, say, a restaurant, when the waitress runs to your table and then jogs to the kitchen with your order. In an underground railway station, lost and disorientated, and surrounded by sprinting commuters, it is unsettling.

I sometimes wonder if the national mania for haste spills over into Japanese love life. Do they make love at the same speed as they eat a bowl of noodles? Incidentally, I was told that Japanese men have the same inferiority complex about white men's genitalia as white men do about black men's. They do not have views on black men since they do not even think about them in this way. For most Japanese, black people occupy the same unreal place in their imaginations as UFOs.

One final note: 'Dallas', the television serial, was taken off Japanese television after only eleven episodes. Audience figures were too low to keep it. The Japanese simply could not understand how members of the same family could be cheating each other, sleeping with one another's wives or husbands and even killing each other. Arguments over a mother-in-law, a workshy son or promotion in the family business they can understand, but the goings-on in 'Dallas' were a fantasy they could not relate to.

Hiroshige, the Tokaido and the Law of Alternate Attendance

Hiroshigo (1797–1858) is probably the best known of the great Japanese woodblock print artists. He is most famous for his landscape paintings, particularly the collection he made called *Views of the Fifty-three Stations of the Tokaido*. The drawings for them were collected on a journey in 1832 between Tokyo and Kyoto. Hiroshige made the trip as part of the entourage of a Japanese noble family. The party travelled along the Tokaido highway, which at that time was Japan's best-known and most travelled road. For over two centuries it had been used for travelling between Edo (now Tokyo), the political capital of Japan, and Kyoto, the religious capital and home of the emperor, by samurai, merchants, priests, pilgrims and noble lords, subject to the Law of Alternate Attendance. Along the route there were fifty-three post stations, where travellers could buy food, stay overnight and find entertainment. Hiroshige's prints presented a view from each of these stages. The collection was published and quickly became successful, popular art.

The original story of this book started when I was wrapping a small copy of Hiroshige's *Tokaido* as a friend's birthday present. The inside cover of the book contained a map of the Tokaido route, together with the locations of the starting and ending points and the fifty-three stopping stations in between. The beautiful coloured prints, the placenames and the story of the Law of Alternate Attendance caught my imagination and, instead of sending the book off, I kept it with the vague plan of one day retracing Hiroshige's steps.

A year or so later I looked into the possibility of following the old Tokaido route. It turned out that the 320 miles between Tokyo and Kyoto is now one of the most populous areas in the world. Parts of the old Tokaido still exist but, with the exception of two national parks, the landscape is mostly urban.

Some of the stopping stations along the way have grown into large towns and others have been absorbed into their suburbs. A few which are off the beaten track are still small villages. Alongside the old road there is a busy new dual carriageway and the railway lines which carry a *shinkansen* express as well as much slower local trains. Of the scenes that Hiroshige chose for his Tokaido collection, some are still recognizable while others are lost in building and agricultural developments and natural changes to the landscape.

My research whetted my appetite for a trip to Japan but also persuaded me to change my original plans. I chose instead to follow the cherry blossom route. However, the story of Hiroshige and the Law of Alternate Attendence is worth telling. His life story and the story of the Tokaido highway give fascinating insights into the customs of the time and the changes that were taking place in Japan just before it opened up to the West.

> The Eastern City
> I leave. And without a brush –
> To see new scenes
> I take the long road
> That leads to the distant West

Hiroshige's death poem, quoted above, written by him just before he died in 1858, was unexpectedly prophetic since his work was appreciated for its artistic merit in the West before it was in Japan. In his lifetime woodblock prints were collected by the middle orders of Japanese society rather than by high-ranking, influential nobles and he was not recognized as an artist of great standing. He was also an unusual artist for his day. Rather than portraying orthodox themes in the conventional symbolic manner, his work dealt with the lives of ordinary people presented in a realistic manner.

His prints were sold through exhibition in teahouses or shops and popular editions were published many times. The quality of the prints was reduced after each edition as the woodblocks themselves became worn, and later editions were sold cheaply. This made collecting a possibility even for people of lesser means. By the time he was thirty-five Hiroshige was a popular and well-known artist in and around the Tokyo area where he lived. His artistic status was more that of a moderately

successful pop star rather than, say, a famous opera singer.

In the late nineteenth century Europe began to discover the beauties of Japanese art and Hiroshige's work was almost immediately recognized for its extraordinary composition, colour and freshness, so much so that the influence of his prints can be seen in some of the paintings of Manet, Toulouse Lautrec, Van Gogh and others. News of Hiroshige's reception in the West increased interest in him at home and, by the turn of the century, some forty years after his death, he had become a nationally known and appreciated figure in Japan.

Hiroshige's father was the third son of an archery teacher. He married into a family in Tokyo and was given an official appointment in the fire brigade. Jobs of this type were restricted to particular families and were much sought after.

Hiroshige was born in 1797 and given the birth name Tokuturo Ando. His name was changed several times. In the Japan of his day one could change one's name to that of one's employer, teacher, spouse's family or adopted family (a family without a son would sometimes adopt a boy or a man). Hiroshige showed an early inclination towards art and was particularly good at drawing and composition. Before he was ten his father arranged for him to have lessons with a neighbour who was an amateur artist. Notwithstanding this aptitude, Hiroshige, as was the custom, would normally have followed his father into the fire service. This pattern was interrupted by the death of both his parents when he was only twelve. He continued studying art with his neighbour and on his fifteenth birthday applied to join the studio of Toyokuni, a master woodblock print artist of his day. Unfortunately the studio was already full and, as a second choice, he joined Toyohiro, a contemporary and fellow student of Toyokuni under Toyoharu Utagawa. The names are similar and confusing since the pupil of a Japanese craftsman or artist traditionally marks his attainment of a certain standard by adopting a new name. This has to include a characteristic syllable of his master's name and thus sounds similar. All this name-swapping is a nightmare for Japanese biographers and historians.

Hiroshige developed rapidly as an artist; his progress was such that after only a year he was formally admitted into the profession of woodblock printing and given the new name of Utagawa Hiroshige, which includes the family name of his teacher. He then took up a securely paid post of fireman, a position he was entitled to by virtue of rank and family, but continued to work as a designer and artist in his spare time.

This way of life continued for ten years. During this time he married. He described his wife as a gentle, feminine woman of samurai descent. They had a son, Nakijiro, and shortly afterwards Hiroshige resigned from the fire service. He gave the post to a relative so that Nakijiro could take it up if he so wished when he was older. For the next ten years Hiroshige worked mainly in the Tokyo area; he did not as yet make any of the journeys which were later to provide the subject matter for his work and make him well known. In 1832, when he was thirty-six, this changed. He placed his son, still only ten or eleven, in the fire service and, satisfied that Nakijiro was in a secure position, started journeying about the country, drawing for his own prints as well as doing such jobs as painting theatrical backdrops for travelling theatre companies. His first big trip was with a procession travelling from Tokyo to Kyoto escorting a gift horse from the Shogun to the emperor. The road they followed was the Tokaido. He sketched views from the fifty-three stopping stations along the way and from these he published the set of prints called *Views of the Fifty-Three Stations of the Tokaido*.

In the Tokaido series Hiroshige showed himself to be an artist with a precise and clear eye. His drawings are not limited by the ritualized rules of Chinese painting then popular with Japanese intellectuals. He drew with a clear vision of simple humanity that was appreciated and understood by the common man. He broke away from the stylized conventions of his time. The people, buildings and landscapes in his prints are real and recognizable. His subject matter was concerned with the ordinary business of the Tokaido and did not include impressions of the ceremonial pomp of the procession he was travelling with This independent view was unique within the formal order of early nineteenth-century Japan. His subject matter and style reflected a common feeling of change in the old order of things. Hiroshige's Tokaido series of prints portrays the ordinary with extraordinary quality. It made him a popular artist with the people.

Hiroshige died of cholera in 1858 aged sixty-two. He was buried in the gardens of a Zen temple in Asakusa. The following appeared in a memorial print to Hiroshige. It was written by his student son-in-law and successor, Ryusai Hiroshige (II).

The late Mr Ryusai Hiroshige, my teacher, was one of the best pupils of Mr Toyohiro, who was a direct pupil of Mr Toyoharu, the founder of the Utagawa school. He [Hiroshige] did not study long under his master, for he lost him when he was 16 years of age. Since then he did not seek another master, for he had an ambition to establish an independent school. For that purpose he studied hard by himself, and had often to climb mountains and descend to valleys, in order to sketch from nature. Thus he established an independent school of realistic landscape.

Though I am a dull and poor painter, yet I have succeeded to his name, therefore I tried to think of a good plan to commemorate his favour permanently. I have, fortunately, succeeded lately in fulfilling my desire by the very kind help of Mr Matsumoto Yoshinobu and a few other gentlemen, who had been related in art with my late teacher, by erecting in front of Akiha Temple, on the bank of the Sumida River, a stone monument with my teacher's last poem engraved on it.

I am extremely delighted that this has been done.

Meiji XV, Horse Year (AD 1882),
4th month (April)
Respectfully expressed by
Ryusai Hiroshige (II)

THE TOKAIDO AND LAW OF ALTERNATE ATTENDANCE

In 1603 the new Shogun, Tokugawa Ieyasu, established a military government with complete control over the whole of

Japan. The emperor and his court were restricted to Kyoto and their role in the country's life became purely symbolic. The new Shogun was a soldier; he did not care for the fripperies of court life in Kyoto and decided to site his executive government in Edo. He reconstructed the city and improved its fortifications. Ieyasu also feared that Japanese life was being adversely affected by foreign influences, particularly those of missionaries and merchants. He instituted a ruthless policy of secluding Japan from the rest of the world.

This situation of national isolation was inherited by the second Tokugawa Shogun, Iemitsu, who succeeded Ieyasu in 1616. Shogun Iemitsu was an even more ruthless soldier and cunning politician than his predecessor. He understood how to maintain and widen his power and, with the introduction of his political control system, called *sankin kotai* or 'alternate attendance', he ensured that the Tokugawa clan would stay in power in Japan for over two hundred years.

Sankin kotai required each of the feudal lords, or *daimyo*, of Japan's noble families to build a substantial home in Edo and to then spend alternate years in residence there while in attendance at the Shogun's court. The year in between was to be spent on their own estates. Close family members of the *daimyo* were restricted at all times to their homes in Edo and the surrounding district. The Shogun, at one stroke, ensured that at any one time half his feudal lords were under his eye at court and for the rest of the time he could, if need be, hold their families hostage. He also required that each *daimyo* on his journey from his estate to Edo should have with him a stipulated entourage of soldiers, ladies-in-waiting, servants and craftsmen. The size of the entourage was directly proportional to the size of the *daimyo*'s estate. The outlay required to pay for it was designed to ensure the *daimyo* never had enough money to finance a rebellion. The Law of Alternate Attendance proved to be most effective in preventing any provincial uprising or court revolution.

This law also meant *daimyo* had to travel between their estates and Edo once a year. There were five main routes radiating from Edo, and the Tokaido, which followed the eastern seaboard to Kyoto, was the most travelled. It was not only used by nobles from the western provinces but also by normal traffic journeying between the seat of government and Kyoto, the home of the emperor and thus the religious capital of the land.

The Tokaido followed the coast from Edo to Yokkaichi before striking inland to Kyoto via Kameyama, Otsu and the southern end of Lake Biwa. The scenery along the way was both picturesque and rugged. Open sea, land-locked bays, distant mountains (including Mount Fuji), high cliffs, paddy fields and many towns and villages all came in and out of view as one proceeded along the route. It was these changing landscapes and colours and the human traffic on the road that were the inspiration for Hiroshige to make some of his greatest compositions.

The journey of a great lord along the Tokaido was an impressive sight. Nobles were carried in beautifully lacquered palanquins. Attendants bore aloft colourful banners and the marching men and samurai on horseback wore full uniform. The whole effect was designed to illustrate the power and authority of the lord.

A noble procession was heralded well in advance so that post stations and inns could prepare beforehand for the extra provisions, horses and accommodation that would be required. Other travellers who knew of it would also stay clear of the road both for their own safety and so as not to hinder the progress of the lordly personage. The procession was preceded by horsemen who would shout 'Down! Down!' and people of inferior rank were required to prostrate themselves on the ground as the daimyo passed. Anyone foolish enough to show disrespect and to be unwilling to pay homage in this way was literally chopped down by one of the samurai escorting the lord. Even towards the end of the Tokugawa shogunate this rule applied and foreigners, now starting to re-enter the country, were at risk because of their ignorance of the customs of the country. The following story from *Dr Willis in Japan* by Hugh Cortazzi* illustrates the point.

On 14 September 1862 a Shangai merchant, Charles L. Richardson, in company with a Mrs Borraidaile from Hongkong and two Yokohama residents, Woodthorpe Clarke and William Marshall, were riding along the road between Kanagawa and Kawasaki, not far from Yokohama, when they met the train of the *daimyo* of Satsuma who bid them stand aside. Ernest Satow described the scene thus: 'They passed on at the edge of the road until they came in sight of a palanquin, occupied by Shimazu Saburo, father of the Prince of Satsuma. They were now ordered to turn back and, as they were wheeling their horses in obedience, were suddenly set upon by several armed men belonging

*Athlone Press, 1985.

to the train, who hacked at them with their sharp-edged swords. Richardson fell from his horse in a dying state, and the other two men were so severely wounded that they called out to the lady: "Ride on, we can do nothing for you." She got safely back to Yokohama and gave the alarm. Everybody in the settlement who possessed a pony and a revolver at once armed himself and galloped off towards the scene of slaughter.'

Apart from the processions of feudal lords the Tokaido was regularly travelled, like any other road of the day, by a colourful stream of merchants, priests, peddlers, entertainers, religious pilgrims, thieves and con men. They all journeyed on foot since only the nobility were entitled to travel on horseback or by palanquin. These box-like structures, called *kago* in Japanese, were very ornate but by today's standards extremely small. They were suspended from a long pole which the bearers, six to eight of them, bore on their shoulders.

Carriages drawn by oxen were the sole privilege of the imperial court and would normally only be seen in and around Kyoto. This could be the cause of some consternation for the procession of a *daimyo* entering Kyoto. If the *daimyo*'s procession crossed the path of the carriage of an aristocrat from the Imperial Palace, the *daimyo* himself would have to get out of his palanquin and prostrate himself on the ground. This was obligatory even though the aristocrat might be impoverished and have no political power. To avoid this embarrassing situation the *daimyo* would send a guard ahead to offer gifts of money to travelling aristocrats with the suggestion that it was a good time to stop for refreshments.

The Tokaido itself was not very wide and because no carts used it, it was unmetalled. Long stretches were bordered on both sides by rows of tall cedar or pine trees planted to dissuade travellers from leaving the road and to provide shelter from sun, snow or rain. The end of every district or province was marked by a stone pillar which showed the name of the district and of the owner of the land. Distances were also carefully marked as this quote from a seventeenth-century Portuguese traveller illustrates:

There is no need to enquire about distances because all the leagues are measured out, with a mound and two trees to mark the end of each one. Should it happen that a league ends in the middle of a street, they will do no man a favour by making the measurement either longer or shorter, but pull down the houses there in order to set up the sign.

Many rivers crossed the Tokaido and they often presented an obstacle to travellers. Ferry boats were used in some places and in others porters carried people and their belongings through the water on their shoulders. The difficulties of these fords, especially that over the river Oigawa, were the subject of several of Hiroshige's prints.

Good communication was necessary between Edo and Kyoto but this also presented a problem for the Shogun since he wanted to restrict freedom of movement. The solution was to maintain a system of barriers along the Tokaido through which all travellers were obliged to pass. It was a serious offence to avoid the control points and the number and movement of travellers were kept under constant observation. The barriers also ensured that none of the *daimyo* could move any of their families out of Edo without permission. This especially applied to womenfolk and any woman travelling with a procession was subjected to the closest scrutiny. She had to carry a certificate of authorization and to it was attached a detailed physical description to make sure she did not swap places with another woman along the way. The higher her rank the more a woman would be examined and interrogated at each of the barriers. This obviously succeeded in discouraging travel but it also gave rise to many Japanese stories of intrigue, adventure and thwarted love.

Kyoto to Tokyo: The Tokaido Route

I left Kyoto to travel to Tokyo along the route of the old Tokaido highway. It was raining when I joined the train from Kyoto to Nagoya and it continued to rain for the whole journey. The raindrops and grime on the train windows blotted out most of the view. I could see we were passing through a pretty country area of wooded hills and flat rice-growing paddies, but then we entered a flat, urban, uninteresting region and I stopped looking out of the window and started to read a book. The next time I looked we were travelling across another plain. As far as I could see in both directions the landscape considered of low-roofed villages and small towns, rice fields and patches of unused land. Roads, railway tracks and pylon lines criss-crossed the plain. I was glad I had decided not to concentrate my journey on this route and also decided not to get off the train to explore.

The train passed a large neon lit hoarding. It said: 'Love is Needing to be Loved. John.' I considered whether this was John Lennon or John the Baptist and wondered who had paid for the hoarding and why.

Nagoya is Japan's fifth largest city. It was flattened during the war by American bombs and rebuilt according to the best city planning theories of the time. Thus it is architecturally sterile and uninteresting, an undemanding and agreeable place to live in. After a quick look around I took the train out to Mishima. From here I could conveniently visit the Izu peninsula, the Hakone National Park and Mount Fuji.

The railway line followed the coast, but too far inland for me to see the sea. The coastal plain was intensely cultivated. The crops were grown under long half tubes of plastic and hidden from view. Eventually we entered a mountainous, wild and visually more interesting region but quickly descended to the plain again, this time into the Shizuoka area. Here they grow most of Japan's tea and every available patch of land was planted with tea bushes. Shizuoka is itself a modern, large, high-rise town, probably like many other Japanese towns, although I did not get off the train to look.

At Mishima I found a business hotel for the night and left first thing in the morning for the Izu peninsula. The peninsula juts out into the Pacific Ocean. It is not far south of Tokyo and the area is a popular summer resort for the city's residents. Ito, an old spa town on the northeast coast of the peninsula, is where Will Adams, the Bristol pilot who inspired the novel *Shogun*, lived.

Ito is built on the site of a number of natural underground hot springs. In the town there are several *onsen minshuku*, or hotels which offer bed, breakfast and a hot-spring bath. I went to the town tourist office to see if they would recommend one to me and to find the site of Will Adam's memorial stone. After the girls in the office had the usual flutter about dealing with a *gaijin*, they settled down, gave me a brochure in English and found an *onsen minshuku* with a vacant room. I went there, soaked in the bath, changed clothes and left to see the launching site of the two Western-style sailing boats Adams built on the orders of the Shogun.

William Adams was born in Kent in 1564. At the age of twelve he was apprenticed to a shipyard where he studied astronomy and navigation as well as shipbuilding. In 1598 he set out from Holland as chief pilot of a fleet of five vessels heading for the Orient. After a long voyage his ship was caught in a gale and washed ashore off the coast of Kyushu. He was taken to Osaka castle where he was held for many days before being interrogated by Shogun Tokugawa Ieyasu himself. The Shogun was impressed by Adams and his knowledge of navigation and shipbuilding. He appointed him to the post of adviser on foreign affairs and installed him in a house in Edo.

In 1604 the Shogun ordered Adams to build an 80-ton Western-style sailing ship. The construction work was carried out on the estuary of the Matsa-Kawa river in Ito. The Shogun was pleased with the boat and ordered Adams to build an ocean-going vessel. This later underwent successful sea trials. For some reason the Shogun loaned it to a Spanish diplomat who sailed the ship to Acapulco, Mexico. It was never returned to Japan.

Adams was rewarded for his services to the shogunate with a large estate. He was given the status of a samurai and the two swords he was allowed to carry were given by the Shogun himself. He adopted the Japanese name Miura Anjin and married a Japanese woman called Yuki. Anjin and his wife had two children. He continued his life as a pilot and died in Japan of natural causes aged fifty-six.

Back at the *minshuku* the food was indifferent but the mineral baths were good. There were three deep tubs in a bathroom that was shared by both sexes. Only myself and an old lady used it. Probably the other guests were too shy to go in when I was there. The old lady was certainly not embarrassed and unashamedly looked me over.

The next morning it was raining yet again. I bought a brolly and then immediately saw a perfectly good one in a rubbish bin. Japan, I discovered, is a fine place for finding useful thrown-away goods. The Japanese would not think of buying second-hand items and so anything unwanted is disposed of with the household rubbish.

With my new brolly I walked along Ito beach. It had dark, unattractive sand. Near the harbourmaster's office I found the memorial stone to Will Adams. It was set in a small but pretty garden overlooking the sea. The wording on the stone was in both English and Japanese and celebrates his amazing exploits. The scene was slightly spoiled by an old mattress lying in the bushes behind the stone. It was off season in Ito.

I walked back along the port road past racks of drying fish, later to be smoked; the town's delicacy. At the *minshuku* I watched television. Princess Diana and Prince Charles were soon to visit Tokyo and there was much about them on the television. On the programme there was a chef who had invented a new rice dish called Diana-Don and a group of businessmen vying with each other for the best money-making idea for the visit. Later I watched an hour-long programme showing the royal couple's wedding and their life together since. No matter what one thinks about royalty, in cash terms the publicity and goodwill they bring to Britain must be worth more than they are paid.

It continued to rain and I had rather a miserable day wandering around the town. Fortunately the next morning was sunny and I caught a train down the coast for Shimoda.

Shimoda is a small town with a busy fishing port. Like other towns in the peninsula, it is a popular summer resort for Tokyoites. Shimoda has an important place in Japanese history since it was here in 1854 that the first important trade treaty between America and Japan was signed. Japan was bullied into ending over two hundred years of self-imposed isolation by Admiral Perry and his twelve black warships. Three years after the signing of the treaty Townsend Harris took up residence in a village near Shimoda. He was the first American consul to Japan and his supposed affair with a Japanese girl was possibly the model for Puccini's opera, *Madam Butterfly*.

Ryosen-ji is the temple in Shimoda where the treaty was signed. Among the Japanese, however, Ryosen-ji is better known as the home of a collection of explicit erotic art. The temple authorities describe the exhibits as 'Buddhist images symbolizing ecstasy'!

I visited Ryosen-ji just as two coachloads of the ubiquitous Japanese OAP tourists arrived. Japanese tour guides carry large megaphones and tour flags and are authoritarian with their charges. The scene in front of the rather small temple and adjacent erotic art museum was pandemonium as the guides tried to order the OAPs into lines. Two ladies from a nearby shop were trying unsuccessfully to attract the OAPs' attention with wind-up clockwork birds. Of the two they set off, one flew into the temple wall and the other was lost in the crowd queueing to enter the sex museum.

Inside the main temple there were a series of portraits of Okichi, the Japanese girl who was said to have become Harris's

mistress. In Puccini's opera she commits suicide out of heart-break when her lover deserts her, but according to the Japanese she was forced to be his mistress and committed *seppuku* as soon as he departed because of her loss of honour. She has since become a folk heroine and the Hofuku-ji Temple in Shimoda was built especially to provide a resting place for her spirit. Harris, on the other hand, maintained he was offered the girl by the Japanese but refused her.

Hanging from inside the verandah roof of the Ryosen-ji Temple is Okichi's *kago* – a small carriage suspended from a pole carried across the shoulders of two men. There is also one of her shoes in a glass showcase on the wall. They are both extremely small. She must have been frightened of Harris, who was big, foreign and meat-eating. He would have smelled unpleasant to the Japanese, since carnivores have a different body odour from vegetarians.

The village of Kakisaki is thirty minutes' walk along the coast from Shimoda. This is where Harris set up his consulate. It has now been converted into a Shinto temple with a cemetery on one side. It is a cosy, very Japanese place off the tourist-coach circuit. In front of the temple is a rather nice amateurish plaque marking President Carter's visit there in 1979. The karumia tree he planted is still small, in parallel with his reputation. Alongside the plaque is a monument erected by the butchers of Tokyo marking the spot where, under Harris's orders, a cow was killed for the first time in Japan for food.

Harris raised the US consular flag on 4 September 1856. He prophetically wrote in his diary on that day:

Slept very little from excitement and mosquitoes; the latter enormous in size. Men ashore to put up my flag staff. Heavy lot. Slow work. Spar falls, breaks across trees, fortunately no one hurt. At last got reinforcements from ship. Flag staff erected. Men form a ring around it and half past two pm of this day I hoist the First Consular Flag ever seen in this empire. Grave reflections. Ominous of change. Undoubted beginning of the end. Query – if for the real good of Japan.

From Shimoda I took a bus north up the spine of the peninsula to Shuzenji, a hilly spa town and the terminus of a train link back to Mishima.

Outside the bus station was a men's clothes shop with the most stupid example I had yet seen of the Japanese fashion of using a group of English words that make no linguistic sense for

tee-shirt slogans or shop names. This particular store was called Tomato Closet Mode Selection!

I joined a queue for the bus behind several Japanese school-children. They were no more than six or seven years old but travelling without parents. This is quite common in Japan, where there is no fear of child molestation and where the children are well disciplined. Each of them wore a yellow plastic crash helmet and carried a large, regulation, leather satchel. I had thought about buying one for one of my stepchildren but discovered to my amazement that they cost over £100. The children peered at me and as we were getting on the bus some of them 'accidentally on purpose' touched me. Those that had done so showed off to the others and obviously thought they had been quite daring to touch a *gaijin* in the flesh.

The road to Shuzenji was exciting. It zigzagged across the side of Mount Agami and culminated near the top at the Nonadaru spiral bridge, the oddest bridge I have ever seen. It is situated at a point where the mountain is too steep to continue the road. Four massive steel legs standing on a ledge halfway down the mountain side support a double spiral structure that carries the road. The bridge rises up along the edge of the mountain, its outer circumference jutting out over the valley thousands of feet below.

We travelled around and up it over the mountains, then descended into a forested area where there were signs warning of the danger of wild boar. Soon afterwards, passing through a village, I saw one in a small cage in the town square. It was eating a turnip. The poor captive creature looked disconsolate and fed up.

The man at the Shuzenji tourist office gave me the address of a *minshuku* and a Japanese map of the area. He located the *minshuku* but did not tell me how small a scale the map was. I started to walk to the address but after thirty minutes realized that at walking pace it was going to take at least an hour to get there and I would miss dinner. I jumped on a bus, hoping it was going in the right direction; luckily it was. The *minshuku* was worth the effort. I had a small, five-*tatami*, room but it looked out over the hills and there was a hot-spring-fed tub. The place was run by a mother and her daughter. The mother's back was bent nearly double, presumably from years of working in rice fields, but she was chatty and friendly.

The dining room was full of guests at their evening meal. We

all sat on chairs at one long table. This was strange for me after weeks of sitting on the floor to eat.

The next morning was sharp and sunny and the walk to Shuzenji station, which seemed an age the night before, appeared much shorter. For some of the journey the road ran alongside a river. At one point along its course a hot spring emerged from rocks in the centre of the riverbed. Villagers had built a circular wooden shelter around the place and used it for the village laundry.

I took the train to Mishima and the bus to Gotemba on the edge of the Mount Fuji Five Lakes area. From here I made a long bus journey to Kawaguchi, a town on the edge of Kawaguchi-Ko Lake. Here it is possible to take another bus to one of the major starting points for climbing Fuji-san up the north flank. The official Mount Fuji climbing season is July and August when the conditions are not too severe. In April, the time I was there, the snow line is still low and to make a complete ascent proper climbing equipment is recommended. I had only good walking shoes and a set of waterproofs but hoped to be able to go higher than the fifth station where the bus stopped.

Most people climb Mount Fuji in the hope of witnessing a sunrise from the top. This means that they either have to climb up overnight or climb during the day and stay on the summit overnight. It is an arduous climb and the mountain at close quarters is not beautiful. The rock is black and volcanic and there is no vegetation. Only the view looking outwards can lift the spirits. The Japanese say that to climb Fuji-san once is wise but to climb it twice is foolish.

I booked into Kawaguchi Youth Hostel and then walked to the lake. At the eastern end there was a cable car up to the top of a steep hill. From the top there was a magnificent view of Mount Fuji and the surrounding area. I took the cable car and at the top stood looking at Fuji-san for over an hour hoping for a clear view of the summit, but a wisp of moving cloud always hung stubbornly round it.

The next morning it was raining heavily again and the clouds were low. I cancelled my plans to visit Mount Fuji until the next day. I was served a strange breakfast at the hostel. Boiled egg, cheese slices, strawberry and cucumber salad, bread and jam. The Japanese at my table ate their strawberries with their boiled egg.

It rained all day and was still raining the next morning. I decided to miss climbing Mount Fuji and to leave the area altogether. I went back to Gotemba and took another bus in the rain, this time to Ashi-no-ko Lake in the Hakone National Park. Hakone, wedged between Mount Fuji and the Izu peninsula, is a region of forests, mountains and lakes. It is most popular with holidaymakers and the original wildness of the habitat has been sacrificed to their needs, but the area is still beautiful. I wanted to go there to visit the Seki-sho barrier gate at Hakone-Machi. This used to be the most important checkpoint along the length of the old Tokaido highway and here, during the Tokugawa era, the identity and right to travel of every person going to and from Edo had been examined.

To reach Hakone-Machi I took a tourist boat, which was built as a copy of a three-masted English sailing vessel of the time of Charles I, south along the length of the lake. The lake is warmed by volcanic heat from beneath the lake bottom and its water remains at a steady 4° C all the year round. The very English sailing boat felt out of place in the warm water and among the azaleas half hidden in the mist and blossoming cherry trees on the river banks.

The barrier station was smaller than I had expected, perhaps the size of two large barns. Some of the processions which passed along the Tokaido had over 20,000 people and to check the papers of each individual must have been an arduous task. Writing this I was reminded that I landed, after a twelve-hour flight from Tokyo at Kennedy Airport, New York, soon after the United States had bombed Libya. The customs officials took over three hours to deal with one jumbo-jet-load of mainly

Japanese holidaymakers. The Japanese, unused to being treated as suspected criminals, wilted around me in the narrow, dark corridor where we were obliged to queue. Compared with this, perhaps passing through the Seki-sho barrier was not an ordeal.

Near the barrier station, in the town of Moto-Hakone, is the start of a long stretch of the original Tokaido road. I walked to Moto-Hakone in the continuing rain and found my way to the old Tokaido highway. It was narrow and cobbled and led into the hills. The road had been forbidden to wheeled traffic and the road builders had made no attempt to lay the cobbles level. I was fascinated and excited despite the rain, which was now torrential, to be walking over the same road that the famous nobles and priests of Japanese history had passed along. The rain ran down the cobbles in a stream. I met two other Japanese walkers and we took pictures of ourselves with one another's cameras, sopping wet and saying 'Cheese'. I walked for an hour in one direction and met no one else. The return journey was not much fun and I sang 'Singing in the Rain' to keep my spirits up.

At the bus station at Moto-Hakone I changed into my one spare set of clothes and caught a bus to Odawara on the new Tokaido railway line. From here it was an hour by *shinkansen* express to Tokyo. Even in Odawara the influence of Tokyo could be felt. The people looked more fashionable and the service in the station café was sharper than in the provincial areas I had been travelling in.

Tokyo

My train from Odawara ended its journey at Tokyo station. This station and Shinjuku, several subway stops away, are the two biggest railway stations in the world. They are on the scale of small cities and give a taste of a future in which people would live in an artificially controlled environment, above and below ground. Both are difficult to find one's way around since most maps, timetables and signposts are in *kanji*.

I arrived in Tokyo in the late evening. As I sat at a station buffet drinking tea, my rucksack on the seat opposite looked much redder than usual. I was tired and the stimulus of being in the brightly lit and busy station was exaggerating my perceptions. I was wondering how I would cross town to Shinjuku station. From here I wanted to catch a train to Chitose Funabashi, a Tokyo suburb where I had been given the use of an apartment. Without a subway map in *romanji* it would be easy to get lost. A European woman walked past the buffet bar. I went out and asked her for some help. She was English and was able to give me precise directions on how to get to Shinjuku on the subway. Once there I got lost in the station maze before I wandered by good fortune past the entrance of the Odakya line, a private line with a stop at Chitose Funabashi. The private railways do not, as do JNR, mark all the names of their stations in *romanji* as well as *kanji*, but fortunately, once on the train, I remembered to count the stops and got off at the right one.

Chitose Funabashi is a respectable but lively suburb of narrow streets, detached homes with small gardens, tiny parks, one with a miniature jogging track, and one large school. Few foreigners live there but the shops are cosmopolitan. Near where I lived was a bakery selling good French bread, croissants and *pain du chocolat*.

On my first morning in Chitose Funabashi the weather was sunny and bright. I copied my neighbours and hung my bedding in the sunlight over the apartment balcony rail.

There was a barber's shop nearby and I decided to go for a haircut. This was an unexpectedly delightful experience but several times more expensive than a haircut in Britain. I tell the story because it illustrates the quality of the service the Japanese expect to receive and enjoy giving.

There were two barbers in the salon, a man and a woman. They were surprised to see a foreigner in their shop and initially were too shy to speak. The woman was already cutting another man's hair but she stopped when I went in. She, her partner and her customer looked at me quizzically. I sat down in the empty barber's chair and showed the man by mime how I wanted my hair cut. He relaxed when he realized that I didn't want a punk's cockscomb. He put a smock over me and wrapped a strip of soft paper around my neck. Around this he tied the neck of a second smock. No hair would slip down between my vest and body. The barber refreshed my neck and face with a hot towel and then took great care to cut my hair as I had asked. Without my asking he even snipped the hair in my ears and nostrils, a job too intimate or too distasteful for my own barber. He expertly shaved me and then massaged my face, neck and shoulders. Next he placed a hot towel over my face for me to lie under and relax. Finally he massaged my back as I leaned forward in the chair. Before leaving he carefully cleaned my spectacles and handed them to me with a bow. It was a therapeutic experience.

Over the next few days I discovered that Tokyo is an exciting but stressful city. A common sight day or night in trains and buses is that of people dozing. Tokyoites work long hours and on top of this often have long journeys to and from work. For the visitor this is not the case, but there is the burden of finding one's way around and the demands put on one's nervous system by the sheer pace and stimulus of the environment. It is therefore important to introduce oneself to the speed of the city slowly. Foreign businessmen who plan to live in Tokyo for a period of time often do not realize this and burn themselves out early.

On the last Sunday in April at the Yasukini Jinja shrine in Tokyo there is an afternoon of open-air sumo wrestling. The event marks the end of a Shinto spring festival and traditionally the best sumo men in Japan dedicate their services freely. Pre-match rituals are shortened but otherwise the contests are conducted with the usual ceremony.

The wrestlers prepare themselves in open marquee tents around the ring. Each sumo stable has its own tent. The ring is made of clay and marked off by a half-buried straw rope. The rules are simple. The first wrestler to set a foot or any other part of his body outside the ring, or to touch the ground inside the ring with anything but the sole of his foot, is the loser. There is no classification by weight. The lighter men try to overcome their weight handicap by making use of their superior speed and agility. Ranking is based on a pyramid system, with teenage beginners (*jonokuchi*) at the bottom and grand champions (*yokozaza*) at the top. Juniors surprisingly start their training with the same build as ordinary mortals. They then steadily put on weight by eating large quantities of rice with each meal. The life style in a sumo stable is strict and dictated by the stable master.

I wandered from tent to tent fascinated by the size of these enormous men. Some joked with me, others ignored my presence, and one huge fellow bellowed at me for photographing him having his hair done. Outside the tents wrestlers mingled with the crowds. They wore thin pyjama-like pants and jackets and walked barefoot along the muddy paths. Some had women with them. They looked so tiny alongside the men that I could not imagine how they had sex together. The young wrestlers with their soft folds of skin and elaborate topknots looked oddly effeminate, but their fleshy fatness disguises great strength, speed and suppleness.

In the late afternoon the top wrestlers began to arrive in black limousines, a single man to the back seat, which he filled, of each car.

The event was used to give apprentice referees the opportunity to introduce and judge top bouts. An elaborate ritual surrounds the opening and closing of each fight and, to the amusement of the audience, the young officials vied with each other as to who could shout the loudest and look the sternest and most impressive. Once in the ring, the wrestlers loosened up with a movement called *shiko*. They raise, in turn, each leg sideways to waist height, bring it down to the ground and simultaneously slap their thigh. The fight, once started, is over quickly. The techniques are executed with such speed that one needs to be alert to see them. The wrestlers move with consum-

mate skill and their expertise can easily be misjudged by a casual observer.

Sumo is steeped in tradition and ritual but it is also about professionalism and winning. Of the many hundreds of wrestlers few become nationally known. Competition is fierce and Western attitudes to sport are beginning to influence age-old traditions. Even the legendary inscrutability of the competitors has now been breached. Nowadays winners sometimes allow themselves a smile in victory and losers a frown in defeat. The rigorous discipline of a sumo wrestler's training deters most foreigners from joining their ranks. Only two, both Hawaiians, have ever made it to the top. Very recently one up-and-coming young Canadian wrestler, with great potential, has retired from the sport. He found the training schedule and the conditions of life in a sumo stable too demanding and feudal for his taste.

I watched the bouts for three hours, then it started to pour with rain and the field we were sitting in became very muddy. The Japanese carried on watching under a roof created by individual umbrellas but my attention quotient had been passed and I left. My last sight was of a 20-stone wrestler from Tonga in the South Seas throat-thrusting his opponent out of the ring.

One of the most fascinating places to visit in Tokyo is the Tsukiji fish market, but it opens before dawn and business is almost finished by 9.30 a.m., so many tourists miss the opportunity of going.

I decided to make a point of visiting it and one morning took the first train on the Hibiya subway line two stops past Ginza to Tsukiji station. I turned left out of the station and walked down Shin Ohashi-dor Avenue past two sets of lights, turned left again and found myself in the outer market. Tsukiji is Tokyo's wholesale seafood distribution centre and perhaps the biggest, most colourful and exciting fish market in the world.

In the outer, smaller area of the market are stalls and shops providing everything for the catering trade from bonito fish flakes to personalized toothpicks. There are also small cafés, bars and coffee shops serving the fish sellers, buyers and truck-men. They are the places to go for breakfast after a visit to the inner market.

At lunchtime the *sushi* bars here sell the freshest *sushi* you are ever likely to taste. The *sushi-san* prepares it with fish bought that morning. In the winter *sushi* is eaten with hot *saké* – a perfect lunch. The outer market also has several stalls selling Japanese cooking knives, which are amongst the best in the world. They are beautifully made with plain wooden handles. The blades are marked by their maker with his own trademark in *kanji*. For quality, Japanese knives rank alongside the French Sabatier's.

It was just 6.30 a.m. when I crossed the blue iron bridge that leads across a small canal from the outer market to the covered sheds of the wholesale market. The market is at its busiest between 6 and 9 a.m.

I walked past lines of vans, piles of polystyrene boxes and many small boxwood fires, built by the truckmen to keep warm while they waited to return home. Soon I came upon the frantic bustle of the market – over a thousand stalls selling fish. The scene was one of mayhem and anarchy. Streams of buyers and sellers were competing for space in numerous alleyways crowded with men pushing and pulling carts loaded with huge tuna fish or with stacks of polystyrene foam boxes packed to overflowing with ice and fish which still wriggled occasionally. I had to be careful not to be hit by one of the carts or motor-driven yellow trolleys which whirled around in any available space. Stevedores in rubber aprons and boots, towels wrapped around their heads, were driving, carrying, pushing and pulling every-where.

After a time I grew more used to the bright lights of the market stalls in the morning darkness and began to recognize that some sort of order prevailed. There was such an abundance and variety of fish and crustaceans that I wondered and worried how the seas could provide so many different forms every day.

The market specializes in *maguro* (tuna fish). They are sometimes brought straight from one of the Japanese tuna fishing boats which now and again tie up at the dock behind the market, but most of them are flown in from all over Japan, London, Boston and even Africa. The *maguro* are auctioned at 5.20 a.m. every morning. The fish, some of them weighing over 700 lb, are then pushed on carts to the buyers' stalls. There they are manhandled onto marble slabs and sliced into sections with an electric saw. The sections are cut into smaller pieces with a long, very sharp knife. Only at this stage does the buyer know if the fish has the desired high fat content and thus whether he has paid a good or bad price for it.

I saw live sea urchins and turtles, *fugu* (poisonous blowfish), many sizes and types of shrimps and prawns, common herring, swordfish, whalemeat, crab, bonito, sea trout and many varieties of seafood I did not know the names of. There were species that I could not distinguish as either sea vegetable or sea animal and others that were so anatomically complicated it was difficult to see how they operated, to separate head from tail. Many of the crustaceans were displayed already shelled. They looked red, intestinal and unattractive. The unshelled ones, true to their crustacean name, were crusty with growths of host creatures and minerals.

The life of the market starts the night before when trucks from village cooperatives all over Japan start to arrive with their loads of fresh fish. They reach the market and queue to be unloaded between midnight and 4 a.m. Trucks carrying water tanks containing live fish go to the south end of the market where their valuable catch is carefully transferred to aerated holding tanks to await the auction. At around 4 a.m. the trucks leave and the auctioneers and wholesale buyers arrive to look at the produce and discuss prices and quality with the sellers. The buyers examine the tuna for fat content. They will also take a good look inside the boxes of other fish and make sure they are fresh. What they buy and the price they pay are crucial for their profits later in the day. At 5.20 a.m. the auction begins. Tuna fish are auctioned on the ground floor and other fish and seafood on the first floor. Meanwhile, at the market stalls buyers' assistants are clearing up, getting boxes of fresh ice ready, sharpening knives and preparing for the arrival of the stevedores with the morning purchases. Between 6 and 9 a.m., the retailers, restaurateurs and *sushi-san* arrive to buy, chat and catch up on the day's news.

By 9.30 a.m. the pace in the market was slowing down. I left and called in at the Namiyoke Temple just by the entrance to the blue iron bridge. It is a Shinto shrine dedicated to the safety of seamen. I sat in the grounds and ate a freshly baked, bean-jam-filled hot cake, which I had bought from a man with a stall by the gate, and pondered between mouthfuls the fate of the oceans.

Kamakura, about one hour by train from Tokyo, is perhaps the most interesting place in Japan for historical temples and shrines. It is also a prosperous and beautiful town in its own right. Kamakura is smaller than Kyoto and I found it much more manageable. It was an easy place for me to find my way around and I enjoyed using the footpath routes that link the best-known temples. I had particularly wanted to visit Kamakura because it was the birthplace and home of Warrior Zen.

In the twelfth century the military leader of Japan, Yoritomo Minamoto, moved the seat of military government away from Kyoto, where he believed the influence of court life was detrimental to the fighting spirit of his generals and their warriors. He chose to move to the isolated village of Kamakura and established there Japan's first Shogun-controlled military government. Over the next two centuries a number of Japan's most important temples and shrines were built there. The military and the clergy influenced one another to create a new breed of Zen warriors and warrior monks.

During this period Chinese Zen masters were the most esteemed teachers of Zen in Japan. They knew little Japanese and the samurai they taught knew little Chinese. The masters were unable to use traditional Zen teaching methods which involved the study of classical Chinese Zen stories and Buddhist sutras. They developed instead the idea of using short *koan* with short answers. Kamakura Zen has since been called One-Word Zen. Kamakura Zen masters observed that for samurai warriors facing battle their *koan* study had an urgency usually missing from that of an ordinary man. They could die at any moment. Their concerns were no longer with future plans or their material welfare. They thus focused on spiritual enlightenment with an intensity that led to quicker and fuller spiritual fulfilment than that perhaps attained by those with more time to consider the pleasures of worldly matters.

During the Kamakura period there were also women warriors and they studied Zen alongside the men. There are contemporary accounts of female Warrior Zen adepts and military heroines. One such female was Tomoe, a member of Minamoto's own clan. She is described in records of the period thus:

Tomoe had long black hair and a fair complexion, and her face was very lovely; moreover she was a fearless rider whom neither the fiercest horse nor the roughest ground could dismay, and so dexterously did she handle sword and bow that she was a match for a thousand warriors and fit to meet either god or devil. Many times she had taken field, armed at all points, and won matchless renown in encounters with the bravest captains, and so in this last fight, when all the others had been slain or had fled, among the last seven there rode Tomoe.

To get to Kamakura from Tokyo I took the Odakyu line to Fujisawa, changed lines there and caught a train on the Enoden narrow-gauge railway into Kamakura town. This is not the quickest route but it is the most interesting. The small train on the Enoden line pulled three old wooden carriages with windows open wide. The journey was delightful and through the village en route to Kamakura the train ran so close to private homes that the passengers could look over into the gardens and living rooms.

My first stop in Kamakura was at the Daibatsu or Great Buddha Shrine in the grounds of the Kotokuin Temple. Here there is a bronze figure of a seated buddha over 30 feet in height. It was cast in the thirteenth century and at the time was housed in a massive wooden temple building. A hundred and forty years later the temple and Kamakura were flattened by a huge tidal wave that swept inland. The structure that housed the buddha was swept away, but the buddha itself remained unmoved and for the last six centuries it has stood in the open and endured the elements.

There were many school parties visiting the shrine while I was there. I asked a schoolgirl to take a photograph of me in front of the buddha. She called her schoolfriends over for support, giggled a lot and then managed to miss the buddha, which has a base diameter of nearly 100 feet, and myself out of the picture frame. A party of American tourists asked me to photograph them in front of the statue. The women were expensively dressed in French designer clothes and caused a stir amongst the Japanese tourists. As I clicked their camera two Japanese ladies took their own photographs of them and more were queueing up to do the same. The Americans were somewhat bemused at being photographed by the natives rather than vice versa.

The Zeniarai Benten Shrine, my second stop, is called the Money-Washing Temple. The shrine is reached through a stone tunnel cut into a steep rock face. Once inside the temple grounds, one passes through a guard of honour of *torii* gates. They are erected so close together that they almost form a tunnel. Each *torri* is donated by a local businessman wishing for a spiritual blessing for a new financial enterprise. The *torii* gate corridor led to a sunny open area. Incense smoke filled the air. A waterfall fed a small pool. There was a covered, *tatami*-floored platform on which a party of schoolgirls were sitting cross-legged eating their picnic lunches.

Off the main temple area is a cave into which flows a mountain spring. The spring is directed into a channel that runs around the walls of the cave. Here is where the money-washing takes place. I put several coins in a wicker basket, swirled them under the water and wished for my own financial success.

My last temple visit in Kamakura was to the Engaku-ji Temple, built in the thirteenth century by the Zen warrior Tokimune Hojo to commemorate the deaths of both Japanese and Mongolian soldiers killed during the Mongols' attempted invasion of Japan, and to mark his gratitude to Zen for the calm it had given him during the campaign. Engaku-ji also became famous during the Tokugawa era as the only legal refuge for women who had left their husbands. Women who managed to reach the safety of the temple grounds escaped the jurisdiction of their husbands and could seek a divorce. Those caught before they reached the temple could be legally punished and even executed by their husbands.

Engaku-ji has extensive gardens and grounds and numerous sub-temples, but perhaps Shari-den, the Shrine of the Sacred Tooth of the Buddha, is the most interesting to visit. It is built in the Chinese style popular during the Kamakura era (1192–1333). The roof corners turn upwards like the toes of a sultan's slippers to reveal ornately carved eaves. This heavy but impressive roof sits uneasily on a simple wooden single-storey base which houses 'the tooth'. I wanted to see this relic of the

Buddha's human form but it was not on display. There are in fact so many temples in Southeast Asia which claim to possess a part of the Buddha's anatomy that if all the pieces were put together they would make at least two complete skeletons.

In the garden of the quarters of the head priest there are 100 small sculptures of Kanzeon, the Bodhisattva of mercy and compassion. They stand on a low stone platform that runs around the perimeter of the garden walls. The sculptures have been worn by the weather and on some of them the facial features had eroded almost completely. Originally each had a different face representing the many sides of Kanzeon's character. Visitors make offerings of small coins to their favourite Kanzeon image. A few of the sculptures had many neat piles of coins while one or two had none at all. Attaching an anthropomorphic element to my choice, I placed a few coins at the feet of a statue bare of gifts.

Of most importance to visitors to Engaku-ji who are interested in Zen is the fact that the temple monks organize an extensive programme of Zen training and events for students at all levels. In the temple grounds there is a *za-zen* hall especially for laity trainees. The authorities do ask that initial inquiries are made in Japanese, however.

Before I left England a friend had asked me to buy him a Kanzeon figure in Japan. Because Kanzeon expresses the qualities of both man and woman it is a potent image for the ideals of Zen development in the West.

I found a small shop in the backstreets of Kamakura selling temple antiques and religious artefacts. They had a small carved wooden Kanzeon figure in the window. I went in. An old man in a threadbare kimono was sitting on a tiny *tatami* platform. A monk and a man in a suit stood near him. The old man had a samurai sword in his hands. He was testing the cutting edge with his thumb. The weapon was obviously valuable and they were in the midst of a discussion of its worth and selling price. The old man was the proprietor of the shop. Despite the two customers drawing his attention to my presence, he ignored me. Finally I asked loudly about the cost of the Kanzeon figure in the window. He got up then to serve me. The figure was overpriced but it was the only one I had seen. I agreed to take it. Much to the embarrassment of his two customers, the old man then wrapped the figure in the clumsiest way I had experienced in Japan. No neat edges on the wrapping paper or beautiful bows made with coloured ribbon. I asked for the figure to be put in a box and to be rewrapped. He did this and then, to my surprise, he offered me tea. The monk called me Kanzeon-san and laughed. He asked if I would like to hold the sword.

Samurai from the ruling class used to be apprenticed to masters of archery and swordsmanship. They toughened their bodies and minds with strict training schedules and demanded equipment to match the skills they developed. As a result of this demand there emerged a group of artist craftsmen who manufactured swords and armour which combined beauty and functionalism to the highest degree. They developed a technical mastery that far surpassed Western methods of the day, and the skill of Japanese swordmakers was so great that the swords became renowned throughout the world. The steel used in thirteenth-century Japanese swords was not matched for toughness or hardness in the West until well after the Industrial Revolution.

For the main core of the blade the swordsmith used a soft, laminated steel which was flexible and tough. The exterior was made of a combination of hard steels which were hammered together, folded over, hammered again and so on, many times over. This technique formed a skin over the inner blade that was composed of thousands upon thousands of layers of different grades of hard steel welded together. The blade was then hardened even more by heating and cooling. Finally it was coated with clay, leaving only the cutting edge exposed. The clay-coated blade was then heated to the correct temperature and plunged into a tub of cold water. The cutting edge was cooled instantly and became so hard that, once honed, it retained its razor sharpness despite repeated use. The part of the blade covered in clay cooled at a slower rate and retained the perfect degree of softness and flexibility necessary to give the blade 'feel' and durability.

For the samurai his sword was not just a weapon but the material symbol of his honour, and he invested it with a spiritual power and surrounded its use with elaborate ritual. To make a binding oath a samurai swore on his sword. Swords that had been through many battles became objects of reverence and worship. They were passed from father to son as tokens of loyalty. If he was beaten in battle a warrior would pray that his sword might regain its lost spirit. At the birth of a samurai a sword was placed by the newborn baby and at his death a sword was laid by his corpse.

Because a samurai sword was held to have such spiritual significance the task of making swords was given a mystical importance. The swordmaker occupied an honoured place in society and was required to undergo both spiritual and technical training before he was entrusted with the job. Only those with the purest of hearts and the highest moral standards could become master swordsmiths. The making of each sword was analogous to a spiritual journey and the swordmaker would undergo ritual purification and fasting before he began to make a sword. While at the anvil he wore white robes and adopted the life style of a monk.

The actual use of the swords was more mundane and bloody. They were fitted with long hilts and were wielded with both hands. A good sword could easily lop off an arm, a leg or a head, and the best could cut through armour and even slice a man in two at one stroke.

To test a new sword the swordmaster or samurai would obtain a corpse or in some cases a condemned man of low rank. The body, dead or alive, would be hung up and various cutting strokes of different degrees of difficulty would be tried out. Each cut had a name and there was even a table listing cuts in ascending order of difficulty of execution. The simplest cut was 'cutting the sleeve' or chopping a hand off at the wrist. The most difficult was a 'pair of wheels' which required the body to be chopped in half by a stroke across the hips.

In battle, cutting off an opponent's head was the most strived-for stroke. The head was taken as a war trophy if the victim had fought with sufficient bravery and was of high enough rank. Samurai who balanced their trust in fate and their own skills with a realistic judgement of the enemy wore steel anti-decapitation collars. Just in case he was unsuccessful in battle, a samurai would burn incense in his helmet before the fight to ensure his head would smell sweet for his honourable enemy!

Practising swordsmanship became one of a samurai's prime occupations, since not only did his life depend on his skill but his mastery of the weapon was equated with his moral and personal development. The best swordsmen became extraordinarily skilful and there are many records of a master singlehandedly defeating six of seven opponents at once or killing a dozen men consecutively in battle.

*

Before leaving Kamakura I visited the beach. It was long, wide and only slightly littered. The sea was dotted with windsurfers. I stripped, except for a pair of shorts, left my bag and clothes by the sea wall and ran barefoot along the sand. It was exhilarating to feel the wind on my body. I passed a large notice board with the warning: 'Tsunami: Caution. In case of earthquakes be cautious of tsunami [tidal waves].' I was reminded of those pointless roadsigns, 'Beware of falling rocks'.

The journey to Kamakura was my last trip in Japan. I spent the next few days in Tokyo finishing off notes and writing to people I had to thank for their hospitality to me. Thank-you gifts and notes are important to the Japanese. As I left Tokyo on the journey home I was glad to be leaving because I was missing my family, but I also knew I would miss the sense of security that being in Japan gave me and the clearly defined sense of purpose that being on a journey gives one.

On my way to Narita airport I visited Nihonbashi Bridge, the first subject of Hiroshige's Tokaido series. It is now a busy city bridge on a main highway. Overhead runs a four-lane flyover. Its concrete pillars stand in the now still waters of the river. On the bridge is a memorial stone to Hiroshige with a brass etching of his Nihonbashi print. Alongside the memorial, on the day I was there, stood a Japanese man dressed in a gentleman's day kimono and wooden gita sandals. He stood motionless, holding a box for offerings. Only his lips moved. I think he was chanting the Amida (Pure Land) Sutra. I took his photograph and put some money in his box, then left to catch the plane for New York en route to England.

The Three-Legged Cauldron

There is a cyclic character to the history of Japanese culture which seems to follow a particular three-phase pattern. First, there is a time when the country opens itself to outside influences, such as those from China between the sixth and ninth centuries and the West between the sixteenth and seventeenth centuries. During these periods the Japanese tend to underrate traditional Japanese values and qualities, although never completely letting go of them. This phase is followed by a period of reassessment and consolidation, during which some imported notions are jettisoned and others are subtly altered, acquiring a distinctly Japanese feel. The third stage is a withdrawal from the outside world. The Japanese shut themselves off from the rest of the world and settle down to a life of regularity and security, safe from the risks created by innovative thinking. This cycle has repeated itself throughout Japanese history and continues into our own time. Japan is now in the middle of the first phase of another one of the cycles. As in the past, it has opened itself wide to Western ideas and culture, while at the same time seeming to ignore or demean that which is best in its own. Japanese businessmen are the new pin-striped colonists and Japanese tourists are ubiquitous visitors to the international tourist traps.

According to the experiences of the past, this present phase of the cycle will be followed by a new period of retreat and retrenchment when the motherland will again become a haven in which to escape the barbarians of the outside world. If it happens, the Japanese may not be as successful this time in burying their heads in Japanese soil. The Western, and particularly American, view of life may have taken too strong a hold on the national psyche. The situation reminded me of a story in

Essays in Idleness,* a book of anecdotes written by an anonymous Buddhist priest who lived in the fourteenth century. Here is the story.

A farewell party was being offered for an acolyte about to become a priest, and the guests were all making merry when one of the priests, drunk and carried away by high spirits, picked up a three-legged cauldron nearby, and clamped it over his head. It caught on his nose, but he flattened it down, pulled the pot over his face, and danced out among the others, to the great amusement of everyone.

After the priest had been dancing for a while he tried to pull the pot off, but it refused to be budged. A pall fell over the gathering, and people wondered blankly what to do. They tried one thing and another, only succeeding in bruising the skin around his neck. The blood streamed down, and the priest's neck became so swollen that he had trouble breathing. The others tried to split the pot, but it was not easily broken and the reverberations inside were unbearable. Finally, when all else had failed, they threw a thin garment over the legs of the pot, which stuck up like horns and, giving the priest a stick to lean on, led him off by the hand to a doctor in Kyoto. People they met on the way stared at this apparition with unconstrained astonishment.

The priest presented a most extraordinary sight as he sat inside the doctor's office, facing him. Whatever he said came out as an unintelligible, muffled roar. 'I can't find any similar case in my medical books,' said the doctor, 'and there aren't any oral traditions either.' The priest had no choice but to return to the Ninnaji, where his close friends and his aged mother gathered at his bedside, weeping with grief, though the priest himself probably could not hear them.

At this point somebody suggested, 'Wouldn't it be better at least to save his life, even if he loses his nose and ears? Let's try pulling the pot off with all our strength.' They stuffed straw around the priest's neck to protect it from the metal, then pulled hard enough to tear off his head. Only holes were left to show where his ears and nose had been, but the pot was removed. They barely managed to save the priest's life, and for a long time afterwards he was gravely ill.

Western influence is like the three-legged cauldron. It is now clamped firmly on the head of the Japanese nation and any attempt to remove it will be very painful. It should be added, however, that since the sixteenth century Western visitors to Japan have been saying the same thing, and the Japanese continue to prove them wrong.

*Translated by Donald Keene, Columbia University Press, 1967.

Zen Buddhism

Zen Buddhism has been practised in Japan for over a thousand years and during that time it has significantly influenced Japanese life and culture. My understanding of Zen is naturally conditioned by my Western background, but I hope that the following short account of its meaning, history and development will be helpful to readers new to Zen. Much of this chapter is based on a chapter in *The Fighting Arts, Choosing the Way*.*

Zen is not about the tea ceremony or flower arranging or archery or the martial arts or even motorcycle maintenance, it is primarily about compassion – compassion for all sentient beings including oneself. This compassion develops through the recognition of one's own true nature, which is the same essential nature as that of all sentient beings and of all things in the cosmos. In Buddhism essential nature is called 'Buddha nature' or 'suchness' or 'one mind'; more specifically, in the Zen school of Buddhism it has been called 'the one hand' or 'one's original face' or 'nothingness'. Complete understanding of one's Buddha nature is 'enlightenment'.

At a human level understanding one's own true nature leads to an active acceptance of one's ordinary life and a recognition of its extraordinary quality. Everyday activities are vested with the same importance as worldly ambition. When asked by a monk, 'What is the meaning of Zen?' the Zen master replies, 'Have you had your breakfast?'

'Yes,' says the monk.

'Then wash your bowl,' says the master.

In Zen the historical Buddha, also called Sakyamuni (his

---

*Compiled by David Scott and Mike Pappas, and edited by David Scott, Rider Books, 1986.

128

tribal name) or Guatama or Siddartha (his personal names), should not be confused with mythical buddhas (symbolizing qualities such as compassion, anger, etc.) and other enlightened human beings also called Buddha by the followers. The Buddha postulated that the way to achieve human happiness and the elevation of suffering is to accept the Four Noble Truths and to follow the Eightfold Noble Path and the Middle Way. The Four Noble Truths are: Life is mainly suffering; Suffering is caused by desire for the wrong things; The way to stop suffering is to stop desire; The way to stop desire is to follow the Eightfold Noble Path.

These Four Noble Truths, or at least their interpretation (since the Buddha's teachings were not written down until about five hundred years after his death), were later disputed by some Buddhists and are not necessarily accepted by all Zen masters. This is not as out of keeping with the Buddha's teachings as it may at first appear. The Buddha had no intention of creating a rigid system of beliefs and certainly not a religious system. That no truths need to be slavishly adhered to is contained in the following advice given by the Buddha and recorded in the Paranibbana Sutra:

Be for yourselves your own flame and support. Let the truth be your flame and support, do not seek any other support. He who, from this moment, or after I have disappeared, is his own flame and his own support, will be a real disciple of mine, a disciple who knows how to conduct himself well.

Many of the Buddha's successors emphasized specific aspects of his teachings, but the particular importance they attached to these reflected personal beliefs rather than universal truths.

The Eightfold Noble Path has generally been accepted in Zen teaching as providing an excellent structure in which to lead a life in tune with Zen ideals. It recommends rightness in: (1) understanding, (2) speech, (3) aspiration, (4) behaviour, (5) livelihood, (6) effort, (7) attentiveness and (8) concentration. The definition of rightness leaves the meaning of the Eightfold Noble Path open to much debate.

The Middle Way is the path that treads a balance in life, and moderation is the quality to cultivate. Moderation in moderation is also important, hence the occasional stories of Zen masters getting blind drunk!

In practical terms the Zen master will not be interested in the

129

personal views of his students on Buddhist beliefs. With faith in their own possible enlightenment and the motivation to practise sitting meditation (*za-zen*) with conviction and determination, he knows that his students will come naturally to follow the Eightfold Noble Path and the Middle Way.

After his enlightenment the Buddha spent the rest of his life (forty-nine years) as a monk, walking from place to place, preaching his philosophy of life. He was the First Patriarch and his successor, a monk called Mahakasyapa, the Second Patriarch. The story of the succession of Mahakasyapa is traditionally the earliest record of a Zen expression of truth. The story is related by D. T. Suzuki in his book *Essays in Zen Buddhism*:*

The Buddha was one day on the Mount of Vultures, preaching to a congregation of disciples. He did not resort to a long verbal harangue to explain the subject he was treating. He simply raised up before the assembly a bouquet of flowers that one of his disciples had offered to him. Not a word left his mouth. No one understood the meaning of this attitude except the venerable Mahakasyapa who smiled serenely at the Master, as if he fully understood the meaning of this silent teaching.

The Buddha, noticing this, solemnly proclaimed: 'I have the most precious spiritual treasure which at this moment I am transmitting to you, O venerable Mahakasyapa.'

Mahakasyapa had obviously realized that a flower expressed reality in ways that words could not. The story may or may not be true, but it probably became popular in Zen folklore because it clearly illustrates the non-intellectual approach of later Zen masters.

Through followers like Mahakasyapa the Buddha's teachings continued to spread throughout India after his death, but nothing was ever written down and for the next four to five hundred years transmission of Buddhist ideas was by word of mouth. Once the teachings were written down in the form of sutras (a sutra is a text which Buddhists believe reflects the direct teachings of the Buddha himself, although in Indian religion generally a sutra is the writing of any great master), unacknowledged divisions in Buddhist schools of thought became more obvious. A major split started about four centuries after the Buddha's death and out of it came two major schools of Buddhist thought: the Hinayana or Small Vehicle school and the

*Rider, reissued 1986.

Mahayana or Great Vehicle school. The former attached much importance to Buddhist texts, orthodox views, rituals and the belief that enlightenment was only possible after extinguishing all worldly needs. The Mahayana school was more open to other influences: it placed little emphasis on texts and rituals, and encouraged participation in the world, while at the same time practising non-attachment. Its adherents thought desires should be mastered and tamed rather than extinguished, and that suffering should be endured, experienced and learned from rather than escaped. Mahayana Buddhism was the school of thought that spread to China and influenced or catalysed the formation of the Buddhist school of Ch'an, later to be called Zen in Japan. *Ch'an* is a Chinese word deriving from the Indian word *dhyana*, meaning the idea of a meditational way of life in which the present moment is lived with full attention and awareness. 'Zen' is the Japanese pronunciation of the Chinese symbol for *Ch'an*.

In about AD 520 the Buddhist monk Bodhidharma arrived in China from India. He was the twenty-sixth Buddhist Patriarch and became the First Zen Patriarch. It was the arrival of Bodhidharma that marked the beginning of Ch'an and the true start of the history of Zen. He travelled to Nanking, where he is said to have met the Chinese emperor Wu-ti. Emperor Wu was a devout Buddhist who had built many temples and, in accordance with the teachings of his time, assumed he had gained much merit. He was happy to meet this well-known monk and wanted him to know of his spiritual achievements. They are said to have had the following conversation:

The Emperor said, 'I have built many temples, copied innumerable sacred sutras and initiated many monks since becoming Emperor. Therefore I ask you what is my merit?'

Bodhidharma replied, 'None whatsoever.'

The Emperor persisted and said, 'Why no merit?'

The monk replied, 'Doing things for merit has an impure motive and will bear only the puny fruit of rebirth.'

The Emperor, a little put out, then asked, 'What then is the most important principle of Buddhism?'

The monk replied, 'Vast emptiness, nothing sacred.'

The Emperor, by now bewildered, then asked, 'Who is it that now stands before me?'

Bodhidharma replied, 'I don't know.'

Realizing that the emperor was not yet ready for his teaching, the monk left the palace and travelled to the mountains, where he became known as Pi-Kuen, the Wall Gazer. He is said to have practised intense meditation for nine continuous years. His wisdom and dedication attracted many followers and through his influence the Ch'an sect developed.

Zen continued to thrive in China after the death of the First Patriarch but Zen monks still followed the Indian way of wandering from place to place and begging for their needs. This started to change with the Fourth Patriarch, Tao-hsin, who settled down in a mountainous area of north China and by the time of his death was surrounded by many followers. By the time of the Fifth Patriarch, Hung-jen (601–74), up to a thousand monks were studying Zen in this same area. It became obvious that in the difficult climatic conditions of this not very fertile part of the country the monks had to become self-sufficient in both food and fuel. Hung-jen's followers built monastery buildings and started to cultivate the land. This was the start of the important Zen tradition that, in the search for enlightenment, both practical and spiritual activities have to be combined. The idea was more clearly formulated by the master Pai-chang (749–814), who introduced the famous Zen expression 'If one does not do any work for a day, one should not eat for a day.' He developed a set of guidelines for monastic life which emphasized austerity and simplicity but at the same time avoided inflexibility and too much attention to rules and regulations. Towards the end of his life Pai-chang still worked in the fields every day. Tradition has it that his followers, fearing for his health, hid his tools so that he could not work. Pai-chang refused to eat until the tools were returned and then did his normal stint.

During the time of the T'ang dynasty (618–907) several great masters formed their own schools of Ch'an. Two of the most successful were Lin-chi (born 867) and Ts'ao-tung (born 800). These schools of thought were later transmitted to Japan by two Japanese monks, Eisai (1141–1215), founder of the Rinzai school, and Dogen (1200–1253), founder of the Soto school. Rinzai (Japanese for Lin-chi) and Soto (Japanese for Ts'ao-tung) are the most popular schools of Zen in contemporary Japan. Rinzai Zen emphasizes practice on a *koan* (a paradox or problem not solvable by rational thought) and Soto Zen emphasizes sitting meditation (*za-zen*), although both schools use both techniques.

Dogen, the founder of the Soto sect, was born in 1200. His father was an aristocrat but he died when Dogen was two, and Dogen's mother died five years later. Dogen was looked after by relatives and, at the age of thirteen, went to live with an uncle, a devout Buddhist, who practised a meditative way of life. This experience confirmed in Dogen his decision to become a monk. Some years later he joined the monastery of Kenninjo, founded by Eisai, and studied with Eisai's successor, Master Myozen. During his time at the monastery Dogen received his *inka*, the seal of a master, but according to his writings he had still not resolved in himself a basic dilemma. He was bothered by the apparent contradiction that if all human beings are born with Buddha nature, why is it so hard for them to experience the authenticity of this reality?

Dogen's doubts led him to China where he studied with Master Ju-ching of the Ts'ao-tung school (called Soto in Japanese). Here he discovered the original teachings of Hsui-neng (the Sixth Zen Patriarch) that *za-zen* was not just sitting quietly but an actual conscious opening-up of oneself to an experience of true reality. Dogen later taught that *za-zen* is not a meditational practice in which the sitter waits for enlightenment, but that the sitting is itself an expression of innate Buddha nature. Without striving the practitioner will, when the time is right, experience in its totality the fullness of pure Buddha nature. Hence, enlightenment is not something to strive for in a conscious way, since this will have a retrogressive effect. Only mental and physical silence produces the transparency in being that provides the right conditions for an illuminating experience of Buddha nature.

Thus *za-zen* is not just being seated physically but also mentally. *Za* is the physical part of sitting, the physical posture. The *zen* part is the settling or sitting of the mind. Hui-neng taught that *za* is when external objects no longer cause the thoughts to run or the mind to busy itself. That is, in practical terms, when we remain calm in spite of external events. *Zen* is to see into one's own true nature, and for this experience of truth to remain completely in one's understanding even in the middle of inner turmoil and passion.

Dogen returned to Japan and, contrary to traditional practices, he returned empty-handed, carrying no sacred objects or translations of new status. He took with him instead a conviction in the power of *za-zen* as a tool for experiencing enlightenment. He believed that man is already enlightened, that we are all liberated equally, but that we do not realize it. Dogen also placed great emphasis on the detail of daily activities and saw each moment as an opportunity to express gratitude for our Buddha nature. He acknowledged the value of *koan* practice but not to the extent of the Rinzai school.

In 1236 Dogen started his own temple and his reputation and stature as a religious teacher grew. Today he is revered as one of Japan's greatest historical figures. He would have nothing to do with the military or aristocratic power struggles of his day and this, combined with his belief in the efficacy of physical work, resulted in Soto Zen becoming the Zen of the people. Today Soto Zen is still seen as the school of Zen most likely to attract the non-intellectual.

The Rinzai school places emphasis on sudden enlightenment (as opposed to the gradual enlightenment of the Soto school), brought about by long practice of a *koan* exercise. This sudden flash of awareness is brought about by intense concentration on the *koan* over a long period of time under stress. Thus the word 'sudden' does not mean that enlightenment is possible without hard work or preparation: rather there are no degrees of enlightenment, either you are or you are not. The mature student is just as far away as the novice in his experience of enlightenment. He does, however, have greater potential for achieving it. One might say that potential accumulates with practice. The *koan* forces the student into extreme concentration on one thought or question that has no logical answer. It compels the cessation of rational thought processes and stops the mind from repeating its usual conditioned responses. This gives space for an experience of the reality that underlies all existence.

There are many *koan*; perhaps the most famous are 'What is the sound of one hand clapping?' and 'Show me your face before your mother and father met', although the *koan* most often used in Zen practice is the Mu *koan*.

A monk asked the master Joshu, 'Does a dog have Buddha-nature or not?'

Joshu replied, 'Mu!'

Mu is a word that has no meaning in Japanese. The problem is: What is the meaning of Mu?

There is no obviously logical answer to this problem. Instead, the answer must illustrate that the true essence of Mind or

Buddha has been experienced by the student. Thus the answer may not even be verbal.

Two contemporary Zen masters have the following to say about the Mu *koan*. According to Yasutani-Roshi:

You must concentrate day and night, questioning yourself about Mu through every one of your 360 bones and 84,000 pores. . . . What this refers to is your entire being. Let all of you become one mass of doubt and questioning. Concentrate on and penetrate fully into Mu. To penetrate into Mu is to achieve this unity by holding to Mu tenaciously day and night! Do not separate yourself from it under any circumstances! Focus your mind on it constantly. Do not construe Mu as nothingness and do not conceive it in terms of existence or nonexistence. You must not, in other words, think of Mu as a problem involving the existence or nonexistence of Buddha nature. Then what do you do? You stop speculating and concentrate wholly on Mu – just Mu!

And according to Katsuki Sekida in his excellent book *Zen Training*:*

Now, 'Mu' means 'nothing' and is the first koan in Zen. You might suppose that, as you sit saying 'Mu', you are investigating the meaning of nothingness. But that is quite incorrect. It is true that your teacher, who has instructed you to work on Mu, may repeatedly say to you, 'What is Mu?' 'Show me Mu,' and so on, but he is not asking you to indulge in conceptual speculation. He wants you to experience Mu. And in order to do this, technically speaking, you have to take Mu simply as the sound of your own breath and entertain no other idea. Only intensely keep on saying 'Mu,' and when you are successful in this practice, quite without any philosophical speculation, you will one day come to realize that the answer is already given, and you will clap your hands and burst out into a great shout of laughter. If, on the other hand, you start trying to think of the meaning of Mu you will lose touch with immediacy and be left all at sea, drifting about bewildered among conceptual ideas.

My own favourite *koan* is as follows:

Kyogen said, 'It's like a man (a monk) up a tree, hanging from a branch with his mouth; his hands can't grasp a bough, his feet won't reach one. Under the tree there is another man, who asks him the meaning of Daruma's coming from the West. If he doesn't answer he evades his duty. If he answers, he will lose his life. What should he do?'

*Weatherhill, 1975.

The English Zen commentator, R. H. Blyth, answers this as follows:

This problem is a central one in human life, particularly between teacher and pupil, husband and wife, and so on. If we teach, they don't understand. If we don't teach they are dissatisfied. Love is mutual obedience. Also it means teaching the other to love more. If I am always obedient, the other becomes impudent, love being mutual, the other's love simply decreases. Kierkegaard says that we must believe in the love in the other's heart and thus arouse it. Perhaps this is the answer to Kyogen's problem, but we must not expect any results. Simply believe that if we open our mouths we won't fall, believe that if we don't open our mouths the other will somehow understand the meaning of the coming of Daruma from the West.

R. H. Blyth was at one time tutor to the Japanese emperor's son. For his wonderful but idiosyncratic understanding of Zen, see his book *Zen and the Zen Classics*.*

SAMURAI AND ZEN

The Rinzai school was very attractive to the warrior classes in the Japan of the twelfth century. They liked the fact that learning and scholarship might be a block rather than an advantage in the study of Zen. Flashes of enlightenment, quickness of intuition, intense concentration – all these they responded to; no longer did they need to feel inferior to the literary aristocracy. Rinzai flourished with the samurai and Eisai was invited to open a temple in Kamakura, the site already chosen for the new warrior capital. Descendants of the warrior class were to rule Japan for the next six centuries and Zen became the 'religion' of the ruling classes. Hence the much greater influence of Zen on Japanese culture than that of Ch'an on Chinese culture.

Samurai warriors used Zen training to condition themselves physically and mentally for battle. The state of consciousness strived for in Zen results from the stripping away of all ego. But this state which precedes the flash of enlightenment prized by Zen practitioners also prepares a warrior perfectly for battle. Hence samurai warriors used Zen techniques pragmatically. In my view they were not necessarily bothered about the essential aim of Zen, which is to realize one's own Buddha nature. In this

*Hokaido Press, Tokyo, 1962.

context the apparent paradox of samurai using Zen – which stresses compassion for all sentient beings – for training to kill other human beings can be understood. But in reality I am sure that to use Zen training methods solely for advancing one's technical expertise in the art of fighting, or whatever, is to misunderstand its essence. Of course, the Masters of the martial arts, calligraphy, the tea ceremony and other Japanese arts transcend the requirements of technique alone and express in their work a manifestation of their inner freedom. This is Zen.

Samurai became more interested in this true essence of Zen during the Tokugawa era (1603–1867) of Japanese history. Then there was peace over much of the country. The samurai class had few battles to fight and practice of the martial arts no longer had a real life or death meaning on the battlefield. Instead, practice of the martial arts slowly became a vehicle through which the samurai could express his understanding of Zen ideals.

ZEN AND THE MARTIAL ARTS

This development was a source of inspiration for later Japanese martial artists, including the men who developed and taught traditional karate. Their view was that practice of the martial arts carried out with the right attitude can contribute to the suppleness, openness and trust of body and mind needed to get in touch with our inner wisdom. This in turn contributes to our ability to take the actions most suited to each moment. Committed and wise practice of the martial arts in this manner can also lead to a state of being in which one does not need to use them. Lao Tzu describes it in the *Tao Te Ching* thus:

For one in command [of himself] perfection is to be in a position of peace; if he should engage in combat it is without anger; if he should seek to conquer it is without conflict. . . . This is the ideal of a man who will not do battle. It is the art of using human strength by co-operating with the sky and it is the supreme wisdom.

This idea of being in command of oneself is well illustrated in the following story of Tesshu, a nineteenth-century master of fencing and Zen. A young man who was a keen fencer went to see Tesshu and asked him what was the essence of the way to fencing. Tesshu told him to go to Kannon Temple in Asukusa and to pray for the answer to his question. The young man went every day to the temple for a week and prayed for many hours but received no response. He went back to Tesshu and told him this but added that on his last day at the temple he had noticed written above the shrine the words 'The Gift of Fearlessness'. 'Was this anything to do with the answer?' he asked. Tesshu replied, 'It is. The secret of our way is complete fearlessness. But it has to be complete. Some there are who are not afraid to face enemies with swords but who cringe before the assault of passions like greed and delusions like fame. The end of our way of fencing is to have no fear at all when confronting inner enemies as well as outer enemies.'

Thus Zen training in the martial arts has two main aims. The first is to free the mind of the practitioner of ego-centred emotions such as ambition, misplaced competitiveness and fear; and the second is to train the body to move from the instinctive and intuitive centre and not through the intellect. This centre is in the abdomen (*hara* in Japanese) and the Zen martial artist gives over to this centre the command of his movements. Calculated, logically thought-out moves dictated by the intellect are slow in comparison and open to error. By hard and committed training with the right motivation the Zen martial artist strives to become at one with himself and, in armed combat, at one with his weapon. The difference between technique-orientated and spiritually orientated martial arts is summed up by D. T. Suzuki in this extract from *Zen and Japanese Culture*:*

When the sword is in the hands of a technician–swordsman skilled in its use, it is no more than an instrument with no mind of its own. What it does is done mechanically, and there is no nonintellection discernible in it. But when the sword is held by a swordsman whose spiritual attainment is such that he holds it as though not holding it, it is identified with the man itself, it acquires a soul, it moves with all the subtleties which have been embedded in him as a swordsman. The man emptied of all thoughts, all emotions originating from fear, all sense of insecurity, all desire to win, is not conscious of using the sword; both man and sword turn into instruments in the hands, as it were, of the unconscious.

*Princeton University Press, 1970, p. 146.

The Oxherding Pictures

The path of Zen has been written about in many different ways but one of the most helpful aids of understanding for me is through the pictorial representation of the Oxherding Pictures. These are a series of drawings which tell the story of the stages passed through by a Zen student as he searches for, finds and then lives according to his true nature. In the pictures the ox represents Buddha nature or one's true self. The path charted by the drawings is perhaps analogous to the levels of spiritual development described by Christian mystics. The pictures have been used to illustrate Zen teachings ever since they were produced during the Sung dynasty in China. There are a number of versions of them, but the collection I like the most are by the Chinese artist Jitoku. They first appeared in a book published in 1585. The pictures were accompanied by poems written by another Chinese, Ri-ming, of whom nothing else is known. They are reproduced here by courtesy of Rider & Company from *Manual of Zen Buddhism* by D. T. Suzuki.*

*First published 1950; reprinted 1986.

1. *Undisciplined*

With his horns fiercely projected in the air the beast snorts,
Madly running over the mountain paths, farther and farther he goes
   astray!
A dark cloud is spread across the entrance of the valley,
And who knows how much of the fine fresh herb is trampled under his
   wild hoofs!

2. Discipline Begun

I am in possession of a straw rope, and I pass it through his nose,
For once he makes a frantic attempt to run away, but he is severely
   whipped and whipped;
The beast resists the training with all the power there is in a nature wild
   and ungoverned,
But the rustic oxherd never relaxes his pulling tether and ever-ready
   whip.

3. In Harness

Gradually getting into harness the beast is now content to be led by the
nose,
Crossing the stream, walking along the mountain path, he follows
every step of the leader;
The leader holds the rope tightly in his hand never letting it go,
All day long he is on the alert, almost unconscious of what fatigue is.

4. Faced Round

After long days of training the result begins to tell and the beast is faced
   round,
A nature so wild and ungoverned is finally broken, he has become
   gentler;
But the tender has not yet given him his full confidence,
He still keeps his straw rope with which the ox is now tied to a tree.

5. Tamed

Under the green willow tree and by the ancient mountain stream,
The ox is set at liberty to pursue his own pleasures;
At the eventide when a grey mist descends on the pasture,
The boy wends his homeward way with the animal quietly following.

6. *Unimpeded*

On the verdant field the beast contentedly lies idling his time away,
No whip is needed now, nor any kind of restraint;
The boy too sits leisurely under the pine tree,
Playing a tune of peace, overflowing with joy.

7. Laissez Faire

The spring stream in the evening sun flows languidly along the
    willow-lined bank,
In the hazy atmosphere the meadow grass is seen growing thick;
When hungry he grazes, when thirsty he quaffs, as time sweetly slides,
While the boy on the rock dozes for hours not noticing anything that
    goes on about him.

8. All Forgotten

The beast all in white now is surrounded by the white clouds,
The man is perfectly at his ease and carefree, so is his companion;
The white clouds penetrated by the moonlight cast their white shadows
  below,
The white clouds and the bright moonlight – each following its course
  of movement.

9. *The Solitary Moon*

Nowhere is the beast, and the oxherd is master of his time,
He is a solitary cloud wafting lightly along the mountain peaks;
Clapping his hands he sings joyfully in the moonlight,
But remember a last wall is still left barring his homeward walk.

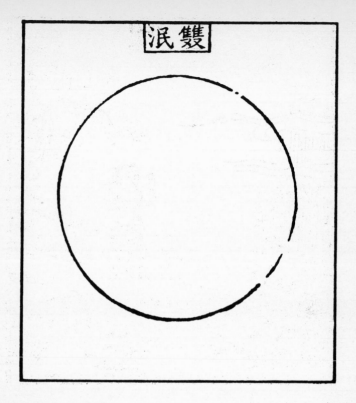

10. Both Vanished

Both the man and the animal have disappeared, no traces are left,
The bright moonlight is empty and shadowless with all the ten
   thousand objects in it;
If anyone should ask the meaning of this,
Behold the lilies of the field and its fresh sweet-scented verdure.

Zen Food

As with other spiritual paths, correct food preparation and good dietary practice form an integral part of Zen training. The philosophy of food preparation in a Zen temple is encapsulated in the style of cooking called *shojin ryori*. This may be simply translated as 'vegetable cooking', but *shojin ryori* carries with it the idea of cooking for spiritual development, and its purpose is to contribute to the physical, mental and spiritual health of the cook and those who partake of the food.

In Japanese the word *shojin* is composed of the characters for 'spirit' and 'to progress' and the complete meaning of the word is something like 'dedication in progressing along the path to salvation'. The Chinese word from which *shojin* was derived was itself a derivative of the Sanskrit term *virya*, which contains within it the idea both of total effort and of self-control, two qualities which are elemental in the Buddhist Eightfold Noble Path. However, the underlying principle of *shojin ryori* is the very simple one of love and gratitude for the food received.

Preparing and partaking of food becomes part of religious practice and takes its place alongside other contributions to the happiness and welfare of society and ourselves.

Shojin cookery had its origins in China and the philosophy underlying it was taken back to Japan by monks who had been to China to study Ch'an. One of the most famous of these monks was none other than Dogen, the founder of the Soto sect. He wrote two treatises on the subject, *A Guide for the Kitchen Supervisor* and *Instructions for the Zen Cook*. They became reference works in many Zen monasteries and the principles extolled also influenced more general developments in Japanese cooking. A number of the unique characteristics of traditional Japanese cuisine have their origins in *shojin ryori*.

In *Instructions for the Zen Cook* (Japanese title: *Tenzo Kyokun*), Dogen carefully explains the qualities to look for in choosing the cook or *tenzo* for a monastery. He writes: '*Tenzo* duty is awarded only to those of excellence who exhibit faith in Buddhist teachings, have a wealth of experience and possess a righteous and benevolent heart. This is because *tenzo* duty involves the whole person.' Further, if a person entrusted with the job of *tenzo* lacks such qualities or the spirit for the job, then they will endure unnecessary hardships and suffering and the work will have no value in their pursuit of the Way. The job of cook, as far as Dogen is concerned, is obviously a serious one.

The same sentiment is expressed by the Chinese monk Zongze (AD 1102) who wrote a ten-volume work called *Regulations for Zen Monasteries* (in Chinese, *Chanyuan Qinggui*; or *Zen'en Shingi* in Japanese). He tells the *tenzo*: 'Put your awakened mind to work making a constant effort to serve meals full of variety that are appropriate to the need and the occasion, and that will enable everyone to practice with their bodies and minds with the least hindrance.'*

Of course, preparing food in the frame of mind recommended by Dogen and Zongze is an extremely difficult task; it requires the cook to concentrate totally on his job. Perhaps giving all our attention to the simplest tasks is the wisest way to start: 'When washing rice focus attention on the washing and let no distraction enter.'

In her book *Good Food from a Japanese Temple*† Soe

Refining Your Life, translated by Thomas Wright, Wetherhill, 1983.
†Kodansha International, Tokyo, 1982.

Yonedu, abbess of Sanko-in Temple, describes the Zen cook's job in very practical terms thus:

It is imperative for the *tenzo* to actively involve himself personally in both the selection and the preparation of ingredients.

The *tenzo* also inspects the rice as it is washed in order to ensure the absence of sand or grit. This he carefully discards, but not without being on constant guard for even one grain of rice that might be mistakenly wasted. He at no time lets his mind wander as he cleans the rice. The *tenzo* also concerns himself with the 'six tastes' and the 'three virtues' (*rokumi santoku*). The six tastes are bitter, sour, sweet, hot, salty and 'delicate' (*awai*), and the *tenzo* works to balance these effectively, while also incorporating the three virtues of lightness and softness, cleanliness and freshness, and precision and care. In so doing, he expresses the spirit of *shojin* cookery. A balance of the six tastes and the three virtues happens naturally when, in the cleaning of the rice, the washing of the vegetables, the boiling in the pot, and in all the other aspects of the cooking process, the *tenzo* commits himself totally and directs his attention to nothing else but the work at hand.

The *shojin* cook emphasizes the importance of simple and nutritious meals prepared from locally available foods. In Japan this would include rice, fresh vegetables, pickled vegetables, sea vegetables (seaweed) and soya-bean products such as *miso, tofu* (beancurd) and *shoyu* (soy sauce). The cook aims to produce from these ingredients food with a harmonious blend of flavours and textures and with visual appeal.

Another important aspect of *shojin* cookery is the consideration of seasonal variations. The Zen cook and priest Keizo Kobayashi, in his book *Shojin Cookery,** describes how a balance of seasonal qualities is strived for by considering the five methods, the five colours and the five flavours. These sets of five refer to the five positive roots of good spiritual practice: faith, meditation, energy, wisdom and memory. The five methods refer to the different ways of preparing food. They comprise boiling, grilling, frying, steaming and serving uncooked food. The five colours are green, yellow, red, white and black (purple, the colour of aubergines, for example, is considered black for this purpose). The five flavours are *shoyu*, sugar, vinegar, salt and spices. The most commonly used spices in *shojin* cooking are ginger root, sesame seeds and *wasabi* (Japanese mustard). By balancing these three sets of five variables the Zen cook aims at

*The Buddhist Bookstore, San Francisco, 1977.

making a vegetarian meal appropriate to the season and ingredients but also nutritious, delicious and lovely to look at as well.

Shojin cookery is also sometimes referred to as *yukuseki* or 'medicine'. This embodies the same principle as that contained in the Indian ayurvedic medical system. In this school of thought food selection and preparation are seen to be inseparable from the treatment of disease and the cultivation of good health. The traditional Chinese medical view is the same: thus, 'if one falls ill one should first examine one's diet, then choose well, chew carefully and give thanks. In this way the curative powers of nature with which mankind is blessed are given full rein to act and nearly all diseases are conquered.'

The Zen diet is traditionally vegetarian and a practitioner abstains from eating all flesh foods, except in particular defined circumstances. This vegetarian practice is based on the Buddhist precept of non-killing of all sentient beings, which recognizes the interdependency and oneness of all life. For a detailed argument against eating flesh foods see *A Buddhist Case for Vegetarianism* by Roshi Philip Kapleau.*

Another characteristic of *shojin* cookery is that no food should be wasted, and even such things as vegetable parings are made use of. The Zen cook thus needs to be skilled both in planning and cooking a meal and in utilizing all the scraps. According to Dogen, the cook should calculate down to a grain of rice how much food will be needed.

Before each meal the Zen practitioner recites a sutra to remind and renew the understanding of the partakers of the food of the path of the Buddha. There are different ones for different times of the day and season and for particular occasions, but the *Gokan no be*, or 'Five Reflections Before Eating', is heard at most meals. *Gokan no be* is chanted in a variety of forms but they all have the same message. Here is the version I am familiar with, it is chanted before lunch.

Leader: We offer this meal of three virtues and six tastes to the Buddha, Dharma and Sangha, and to all the life in the Dharma worlds.

All: First, seventy-two labours brought us this food; we should know how it comes to us.

Second, as we receive this offering, we should consider whether our virtue and practice deserve it.

*Rider, 1983.

Third, as we desire the natural order of mind to be free from clinging, we must be free from greed.

Fourth, to support our life we take this food.

Fifth, to attain our Way we take this food

The first line of the response reminds us of how much effort on the part of very many people went into growing, harvesting, processing, cooking and serving the food about to be eaten and how food may only be grown because of the natural gifts of sunshine, rain and soil. The second line asks if we have acted with enough charity, love and effort at good practice to deserve such a gift. The third line reminds us not to be greedy and to remember by not eating overmuch those people who are hungry. The fourth line expresses the view that food is a medicine needed to sustain physical and spiritual strength. Finally, the fifth line reminds us that we eat to be given the opportunity to follow the Buddha Way and to express our Buddhahood in the world.

Reading, Writing, Language

READING AND WRITING

The Japanese have the highest literacy rate in the world. This had been the case for over a century, and their achievement is impressive given the difficulty of their writing system.

To learn to write their own language the Japanese must master four ways of writing. These are *kanji, hiragana, katakana* and *romanji*. *Kanji* are Chinese characters. The Japanese started to adopt and adapt Chinese characters as a means of writing in Japanese in the fourth or fifth century. It created problems for would-be scribes, since Chinese and Japanese are unrelated languages and have different grammatical and phonological systems. Further, Chinese is based on single ideograms representing whole words and not on an alphabetical system. The result was an extremely clumsy writing system which used the adopted Chinese characters in three ways. First, with their original meaning but with a Japanese pronunciation; secondly, as characters for uniquely Japanese words unrelated to their original meaning; and, thirdly, just for their sounds as a way of writing Japanese. This had the strange result that even today Chinese and Japanese scholars can read each other's language if it is written in *kanji* but are still unable to speak to each other.

To make the writing system easier Japanese scholars in the tenth century developed a syllabary (a set of characters) representing the fifty most common sounds used to pronounce *kanji*. The syllabary is called *hiragana* and is used to connect *kanji* and to write Japanese words phonetically. *Katakana* was evolved at the same time. This syllabary used the same fifty sounds as *hiragana* but the characters are formed differently. It is rather like the difference between printing and script. *Katakana* is used to write foreign words in Japanese. *Romanji* uses the Roman alphabet to write Japanese. Nowadays most Japanese can read and write *romanji* and in large cities one can often see the names of important landmarks given in *romanji*. This is especially useful for foreigners at railway stations.

There are over 40,000 *kanji* characters but in modern times only about 3000 are taught in schools. Newspapers also have to be written within *toyo-kanji* limits. *Toyo-kanji* are the 2000 *kanji* or commonest characters chosen by the Japanese government for use in popular written works. The government is also trying to simplify and reform the Japanese writing system in other ways. They still have much to do, however, and it is estimated that a Japanese student needs two years' more schooling than his or her Western counterpart just to master the technicalities of the reading and writing system. The government has to proceed with care since, if the system is simplified too much, young people of the future will have difficulty in reading literature or academic works that have not been limited to *toyo-kanji*.

For a foreign student of the Japanese language perhaps the biggest frustrations in reading and writing are the multiple meanings and pronunciations possible for the same characters. This is further exacerbated by the commonest characters often being those with the greatest number of meanings. However, spoken Japanese, taught using the Roman alphabet, is perhaps easier to learn, at least superficially, than many European languages.

Societies using an alphabetical system are said to be at a distinct advantage to those using a character system in the development of social change. For this reason some countries such as Turkey have changed from a character system to an alphabet. In Japan, however, moves towards romanization have never been successful, although nowadays the Roman alphabet is part of every school curriculum. Edwin Reischauer in his book *The United States and Japan** even goes so far as to say: 'Perhaps the greatest single misfortune in the history of Japan was that, because of her geographical position, Chinese characters and not one of the Western alphabets became the basis of her writing system.' This and the argument about social change seem presumptuous to me. In fact the Japanese people have been open to social change (although this seems to go in cycles of

*Cambridge, Mass., 1962.

extreme introversion or extreme absorption of external ideas) and, at various times in their history, have been very receptive to foreign influences, as they are now. One result of this is that in the course of time they have assimilated numerous Eastern and Western philosophical and scientific terms and ideas into their culture and language, so much so that in recent times the Chinese have started to borrow back from the Japanese *kanji* characters which have been modified by the Japanese to represent new objects and concepts.

LANGUAGE

Nowhere is the connection between language and culture more easily seen than in Japan in both the way the structure of the Japanese language reflects and perhaps perpetuates particular traits in the national character, and the way the language itself has changed radically after the impact of major social events, for instance, the introduction of Confucianism and Buddhism.

This relationship between society and the Japanese language is most easily illustrated by the way in which Japanese honorific and deferential forms of speech are used. Japanese society is even today hierarchical – almost feudal in some respects – and spoken Japanese contains a battery of expressions which, used appropriately, set both the relative social positions and the sex of the speaker and the person spoken to. Both parties immediately know where they stand on the ascending ladder of inferiority, equality or superiority. For instance, there are three ways of saying Mr Smith. Smith-Sama for a person of elevated rank, Smith-San for a person of the same rank, and Smith-Kun for an inferior or to a casual friend. Within these divisions there are further sublevels. Until the changes following the Second World War it would have been fair to say that there were no democratic forms of speech in Japan. Since the war there has been a slow disintegration of the feudal system and this is reflected by a growing informality of speech in the workplace and especially in the home, where honorific terms are now rarely used. However, judging by the way the Japanese use their language, contemporary Japanese life is still much more hierarchical than in the West. This situation, which goes against the grain of modern Japanese attitudes, is probably sustained to some extent by the structure of the language.

Nakamura Hazime, a professor at Tokyo University, some

157

years ago wrote a number of works on the way the Japanese language has influenced Japanese behaviour and thought patterns. His conclusions were interesting and not all that flattering, judged by Western standards of good and bad. However, judged by his own theory, his conclusions will have been conditioned by his own language patterns, just as mine and the reader's views are by ours. Nakamura said that the Japanese have a tendency to think in terms of the social group they belong to, to think intuitively and irrationally, and generally are inclined to accept the status quo rather than push for change. The results of these and other traits, he concludes, are the acknowledgement by the Japanese of the rights of a group over an individual member, a close observance of family morals and taboos and a leaning towards extreme nationalism. Nakamura suggests that these national characteristics are encouraged by the language because it does not often use a first or second person subject. For instance, a Japanese who wants to say the Japanese equivalent to 'I am hungry' will say 'The stomach has become empty'. This, Nakamura says, results in the Japanese not having a full awareness of the individual or of an independent performer of actions as an objective being.

The Western equivalent to Nakamura is G. W. Grodeck (1866–1934), a philosopher, healer and colleague of Sigmund Freud, who in his book, *The Meaning of Illness*,* states that many problems of Western society are caused by an overemphasis on the first person subject. He says:

. . .consider the strange fact that the classical languages express the Ego only by means of verb endings. For us the 'I' has become an almost insuperable linguistic obstacle to recognising the unimportance of the human individual and to endowing life, religion, poetry with the sacred awe felt towards nature. Whoever looks at modern Europe carefully will be horrified about our lack of culture, no matter how highly he may value the sophistication of our civilisation.

And in another passage he says:

And this brings me back to the statement that language hinders culture. You must recall that language possesses the word I, a word which we hear everywhere and which determines and dominates our whole life. And then you must try and understand what kind of an I this is. Try and understand this I, separate it, grasp it as an entity on its own. You will see that this is impossible. There is no such thing as an I; it is a lie, a

*Hogarth Press, 1977.

distortion, to say, 'I think, I live'. It should be: 'it thinks, it lives'. It, that is the great mystery of the universe. There is no I. Science has long since proved even to the pedants that this I is made up of millions of smaller I's; every day brings more scientific proof of the fact that the blood that circulates inside us is as independent an entity as is the I in which it circulates, and that the human being is as dependent on and inseparable from the whole as is the blood from the human being. Daily, science adds more proof to the notion that every organ, the brain, the heart, every gland in the body, every cell is an entity with a will and a mind of its own, and yet that it is nothing but a part which has come about through the whole and affects the whole. Everything is in flux. Quite certainly there is no I. This is one of the language's untruths and unfortunately a fateful one. For nobody can free himself from this single word I.

Both Grodeck and Nakamura are making the point that, although language allows us to communicate, our thoughts, actions and emotions are in fact influenced by the language we use for their expression. Thus, although language is an essential tool, if we do not work hard at a measure of self-awareness and self-remembering the language we habitually use will condition and to some extent enslave our actions and thoughts. What we view as the real world is in fact in some measure constructed in the unconscious and conscious mind by our language habits. We are programmed to make particular interpretations of events. For me this is a partial explanation of what Buddhist sages mean when they say that the common view of reality is an illusion.

If Grodeck and Nakamura are right, what they say goes some way to explaining the success of Shinto and Buddhism in Japan, with their emphasis on the indivisible unity of man, God and the cosmos, and of Christianity in the West and its stated division between man and God and belief that man is God's chosen being. My understanding is that Buddhism holds that there is no single constant entity such as the 'self' or the 'I'. The present is constantly being created. Moment by moment the present becomes the past and the future becomes the present. Similarly there is no fixed being that we can call the self. The self has no fixed nature; change is ceaseless. Buddhism teaches that trying to fulfil the desires of this changing self is thus impossible. Short-term satisfaction may be obtained but it will quickly be followed by more demands from the self, manifesting through the ego.

In conclusion, the fascinating question posed by the thoughts of Grodeck and Nakamura is: Does a nation's language have a major part to play in creating and perpetuating a particular cultural style? If so, are we as free in our way of thinking as we imagine we are? Is our freedom of will lost as soon as we learn to speak? We use language for communication and normally take it for granted that language is a tool we control. Rarely do we consider that language itself influences the way we see the world and our modes of thought. Our personal view of reality is at least conditioned by the language habits of our particular country and social group. Language also conditions social intercourse and cultural norms, and radical changes in the patterns of a nation's language and its social conditions mirror and influence each other.

Japan for the Visitor

Japan is a complex country, a fascinating mixture of the old and the new. She is also one of the wealthiest and most powerful nations in the world. Her consumer products are the most successful in world markets, her currency one of the strongest, her methods of management and production the most admired and her foreign policies as likely to affect our lives as much as those of America or Russia; and yet few people in the Western world know anything about her, apart, that is, from stories of shoguns, Zen, Mount Fuji, samurai warriors and, more recently, the deadly assassins the *ninja*. A more rounded view of the country is, I hope, given by this book, but of course the very best way to get to know a country and its people is to visit it. Japan is a long way away from Western countries, potentially expensive to get to and, once there, not cheap, but with careful advance planning costs can be less than imagined and the rewards of a visit well worth the effort.

Japan is one of the world's most interesting and practical places to visit for a holiday for several reasons. First, it is unique in my experience in being a modern Western-style state with excellent communications, fast and efficient services, and a successful economy, which is nevertheless free from crime and dishonesty, clean and hygienic wherever you go, as well as being surprising, different and oftentimes, outside the industrial centres, beautiful. Secondly, if you enjoy being on your own and away from other tourists Japan is perfect. In some of the remote regions you could be the first foreigner or at least one of the very few to have ventured into that area. Thirdly, you can move easily between busy populous cities with all the culture and amenities you could want, ranging from contemporary art galleries to Kabuki theatres, hamburger joints to *sushi* bars, and

lightly populated mountain areas with ancient castles and long-established Buddhist temples where you can stay the night for little money.

Getting There

Apex return fares are the simplest and most straightforward way of booking moderately economic flights to Japan. The main drawbacks with them are that you have to decide in advance exactly when you are going and coming back and no stopovers are allowed. Most travel agents can find you cheaper fares than Apex with the more obscure airlines. They are perfectly all right but the journey may take longer because of idiosyncratic flight patterns and stopovers in unlikely places. The tickets are cheaper but otherwise suffer the same disadvantages as Apex. Regular scheduled tickets which allow late booking, open-dated return and some stopovers are expensive and in many cases more expensive than a Round-the-World fare, which is the ticket I would recommend. Different airlines combine to produce these tickets and they give you a variety of possible routes. The only condition is that you continue to travel round the world in one direction only. This does not matter if you are going to Japan since it is almost as far to Europe or the East Coast of America whether you fly east or west. With the Round-the-World ticket you can plan your own itinerary and stop off for a few days or more at exotic places en route. This makes the price of the ticket seem much more reasonable. Different airlines have different rules but with most you can change your flight dates and routes three or four times en route without incurring any extra charge.

Most residents of European countries do not need a visa to visit Japan and they may stay for between ninety and 180 days without applying for one. Visitors from America and Australia will need a visa but they are readily given and are free of charge. Apply to the Japanese Embassy in your country for details.

To my knowledge, at the time of writing visitors from Europe, Australia or America do not need any special innoculation certificates to get into Japan. Once there, you do not need to take any health precautions that you would not take at home.

Climate

Japan is 3000 km long from the northern end of Hokkaido to the southern tip of Kyushu. The interiors of the three main islands are mountainous. The climate differs considerably from one end of the country to the other and from the coastal plains to the mountain regions. Each of Japan's four seasons has advantages and disadvantages for the tourist. Summer is hot and humid in the lowlands, slightly cooler and less humid the higher or farther north you travel. Winter is very cold in Hokkaido and in the mountains, moderate in Kyushu and warm in the Ryukyu Islands. Spring and autumn are the most temperate, but these are the seasons when the Japanese are most likely to go on holiday.

For me any time is a good time to visit Japan. The important things are to check up on the climate and conditions to be expected in the regions where you intend to spend most time and to be prepared. Also be careful not to plan visits to tourist centres during Japanese peak holiday times. Specific information on the various areas of Japan is available from detailed tourist guides (two titles are suggested at the end of the chapter) and Japanese National Tourist Offices.

Getting Around

PLANNING A ROUTE

A problem I had before going to Japan was choosing a route for my journey from all the possibilities that were available. This was made more difficult by the way the various guidebooks divided the country into different regions and used different names for the same area. For instance, Central Honshu in one book was called Chubu in another. Smaller guidebooks with less detail were easier to understand but tended to cover only the predictable tourist places. If you are planning an independent trip to Japan, I would recommend you to buy a detailed map of the country and, with one detailed guidebook, get to know the names, whereabouts, geography and climate of each of the regions before deciding on your route.

TRAINS

Trains are the quickest way of exploring Japan. Japanese National Railways (JNR) run 28,000 trains daily and there are also numerous private railway lines. The fare system, however, has to be understood if you are not going to find it very expensive. There is a basic fare for whichever train you use and this is calculated by the distance you travel. Added onto this fare are various surcharges mainly dependent on how fast the train is, but also on whether you reserve a seat or not and which class you travel. There are four categories of train; the slower they are the less you pay. The *shinkansen* are the fastest; limited-stop express (*tokkyo* or *cho-tokyu*) next to fastest; express (*kyoto*) next to slowest; and local trains (*futsu*) the slowest. For people with limited time and no strictures on their expenses *shinkansen* are the trains to use. For the budget traveller in no rush the best trains are a combination of the limited express for long journeys and the local trains for exploring a particular area.

If you are travelling from A to B and wish to stop at places en route, purchase a ticket for the whole journey; you are allowed to make as many stopovers as you wish, as long as the date on your ticket remains valid for the whole journey. The period of validity is one day for 100 km, two days for 200 km and then one day for each additional 200 km. You can get refunds on unused tickets and also change your routing once without any handling charge. If you are not sure how much your fare is or where you are going, buy the cheapest ticket from a ticket machine or ticket office and pay any balance due at the station you get off at. Most stations have a fare adjustment counter. (Reserved tickets are purchased in the railway station from the 'green window' counters, called *midori-no-madoguchi* in Japanese).

For foreign visitors to Japan who intend to make a high number of train journeys it is worth buying a Japan rail pass. These are valid for one to three weeks and can save the traveller quite a lot of money. They may only be purchased outside Japan. To obtain one and a copy of the conditions of use, apply to a Japanese Airlines (JAL) office in your own country.

Other tips for travelling by train are as follows. Do not carry a lot of luggage; busy trains normally have space for only one medium-sized suitcase. Most trains have a buffet car and/or food and drink available from a trolley which is pushed up and down the aisles. They also sell *eki-ben* (lunchboxes) but those sold on stalls at the station or by the sellers who run along the platform when a train stops at a station are usually cheaper and fresher. All reasonably sized stations and all those on JNR lines display station names in *kanji* and *romanji* letters. The name of a station is in the middle of the nameboard and the preceding and following stations beneath it. Keep a careful watch for these nameboards when approaching a station. Sometimes there is only one and it can flash past before you have seen it. Avoid travelling during the rush hours (7.30–9.30 a.m. and 5–6 p.m.). All major stations have an information counter where you can get maps, accommodation advice and help with your train booking from English-speaking assistants. The subway systems in large towns, and particularly in Tokyo, are complicated and difficult to follow but not impossible. Before proceeding to use them visit a local tourist office, JNTO (Japanese National Tourist Office) or TIC (Tourist Information Centre), or station information counter and get a subway map. Best of all, if possible make your first trip with a Japanese friend.

BUSES

Japan has an excellent network of local city and rural buses and often the bus terminal is adjacent to the train station, so it is easy to make use of buses if you are travelling by train. For long journeys buses are slower and not significantly cheaper than trains and I do not recommend them. They are useful only for local journeys. Unfortunately buses do not show their destination in *romanji* so it is important to sort out beforehand the number of the bus you wish to take, in which direction you want to take it, and where, if at all, you need to change buses. If you do not speak Japanese, this information can be obtained from a tourist office, a Japanese friend or a detailed guidebook, but only with difficulty from a passerby on the street. Once you know your bus number and destination, write them on a piece of paper. You can then show this to people at the bus stop or on the bus and they will be able to help you get on the right bus and get off at the correct stop.

Knowing how much to pay once you are on board is much easier than catching the right bus. As you enter the bus take a ticket from the dispensing machine inside the door. It has a number on the back. A meter above the driver's head matches the cost of the fares against the numbers on the backs of tickets. It rotates during the bus journey, increasing the fare against the ticket numbers accordingly. As you get off, put your fare into the collecting machine by the driver's side. There is a box attached to the machine that will give change for coins and notes.

TAXIS

Taxis are metered and tipping is not a custom so you know exactly how much your journey has cost. Taxis are quite expensive but very convenient for going to a place for which you have no directions or if you are lost. It is a good idea to carry the address and telephone number of where you are staying or going in *romanji* and *kanji*. Then you can show the address to the taxi driver. If he gets lost he will stop the cab and ring for directions.

CAR HIRE

Car hire is widely available if you have an international driving licence, but I would not recommend it. Apart from the rather complicated procedure of hiring the car, the roads are very busy, maps, if available in English, are poor, and the signposts are mainly in Japanese. That is assuming there are signposts; often there are not, and even the Japanese get lost on their own roads on long journeys. It is a mystery and a surprise to me that a country with such high technological capabilities cannot provide a reasonable signposting system for its roads. It is another example of how Japan can continually surprise.

HITCHHIKING

I have never done any but I am told it is easy because it is unusual in Japan and the hitchhiker is a novelty.

Finding an Address

It is extremely difficult even for local people and taxi drivers to find a place in Japan just by its address. This is because there is no logical system of house numbers or street or road names. In fact until the middle of the 1950s houses were numbered by the chronological order in which they were built, not by their location. In many areas houses numbered before the system changed still retain their old numbers, so complicating any new scheme of numbers. Streets do not have names, although some major roads and avenues do; instead, addresses are by district, and within each district each building has a one- or two-(hyphenated) digit number. The smallest district unit is called a *chome*. The largest district unit is called a *ku* and between these two are other units of varying size. Sometimes they are called *cho* or *machi*. Cities are suffixed by *shi* and prefectures by *ken*. This is helpful in distinguishing a city from a prefecture when they have the same name. A Western example is New York City and New York State. Rural addresses may contain the word *mura* which means 'village' and *gun* which is a county, a unit smaller than a prefecture.

The best way to locate an address is to find it on a map of the vicinity. This is made easier by the practice of printing small maps on the back of business cards, restaurant match packets and such like. Otherwise, for a first visit to a place, travel to the general vicinity by bus or train and then take a cab.

Accommodation

There is no shortage of accommodation for the traveller in Japan but none is especially cheap. In the cities there is a wide variety of options and in rural areas small hotels, *minshuku* (a Japanese version of bed and breakfast), temples which take visitors, and sometimes *ryokan* (traditional Japanese hotels). Much could be written on the subject, but for the short-term visitor matters can be simplified.

Hotels are the same the world over and not much need be said about them here. If you are visiting Japan as part of an arranged trip or for business reasons, your travel agent will book you into a vetted hotel. Some offer Japanese as well as Western-type rooms, and if you want a room with *tatami*-matted floor and sunken bath tub, request a reservation in a Japanese-style room. For the independent traveller your choice of hotel will depend on your budget. They range from the international luxury type to the business hotel to the cheap but clean, small, local establishments. *Avec* or love hotels are discussed later.

The very cheapest places to stay are youth hostels. There are quite a number in Japan and their rules and regulations are similar to those in the West. Details and addresses in Japan are available in a booklet from the YHA head office of your own country. Youth hostels are convenient for one-night stays but at busy holiday times they are heavily used and need to be booked ahead.

Ryoken (Japanese inns) provide the very best of traditional Japanese taste, culture and food. They are usually sited in a beautiful spot and/or look onto elegant gardens. The service will be restrained and flawless in its maintenance of correct behaviour. They are very expensive but worth at least one night's stay for the experience. A certain style of behaviour is expected from their guests, but allowances are made for foreigners. A small booklet, *Japan Ryoken Guide*, is obtainable from the tourist section of the Japanese Embassy or a JNTO office in Japan.

Minshuku are definitely the best places to stay for independent visitors to Japan who are on a budget but who do not have to be extremely careful. *Minshuku* are family homes that take guests, and staying in one really gives an insight into and feel of Japanese life. They provide a room, bedding, breakfast and supper. Foreigners are a novelty and you will be treated with real hospitality and warmth once you have established you are sensitive to and respect and understand the simpler of their customs. The most important of these are to remember to leave your shoes at the door and not to use soap in the hot tub. Others you can learn as you go along by being careful and observant as you move around. Addresses and reservations for *minshuku* can be obtained from the information counters found at most reasonably sized railway stations. A detailed list of addresses and *minshuku* customs can be obtained from the Japan Minshuku Association, Pearl Building, Room 201, 10–8 Kyakunincho

2-chome, Shinjuku (telephone 03 371 8120). The word *minshu-ku* is pronounced 'minsh-ku'.

LOVE HOTELS

Because most Japanese live in very small houses or apartments with their families, it is very hard for young unmarried or even married couples to find somewhere to make love privately and out of earshot of other people. The problem also arises for people carrying on affairs which they want to keep secret from family and neighbours. The solution society has found is short-stay hotels called love hotels or *avec* hotels. Such establishments are quite common and their advertisements giving the rates for a 'rest' per hour and details of facilities offered are to be seen in most large cities. The adverts are garish but the hotels themselves are run very discreetly. They are normally surrounded by a high wall and the entrance and exit are separate to reduce the chance of embarrassing encounters. The anonymity of the guests is closely guarded, but the management tries to offer all the facilities needed to allow them to indulge in their wildest fantasies. Even the 'straight' rooms are decorated in sensuous style, with lots of satin, soft cushions and mirrors. Videos with pornographic films are also common nowadays, and cameras are available so that guests can film themselves if they want a rerun of their own action later.

In the cheaper establishments the cost is paid on entry and the money is pushed through a narrow window to a cashier hidden from view. At the better establishments one is greeted by the manager or manageress, who will discreetly discuss your requirements before a maid shows you to your chosen room. She will make the room comfortable and bring in tea and dainty cakes. Adjacent to each room there is a small hot tub for post-coital talking and soaking.

A tip for travellers on a budget: after 10 p.m. the room rates at love hotels are often lower than those of regular hotels. So if exotic surroundings do not put you off sleeping, they make a cheap alternative for a single night's stay.

Japanese Food

It is said that Chinese food is for the pleasure of the stomach, French food is for the pleasure of the nose, and Japanese food for the pleasure of the eye. This is only partly true of Japanese food, which to be really enjoyed should be tasted with the tongue, the heart and the eye. Traditional formal meals are cooked and presented by the Japanese chef with the intention of inspiring both the senses and the spirit of the recipients of the food. Season, location, religious and/or cultural factors are considered before the menu is planned. The food being served and the manner of its presentation then dictate the nature of the serving bowls or plates to be used. Ceramic, wood or lacquer tablewear is selected for each dish according to which harmonizes most aesthetically with the colour, texture and appearance of the food. In the centre of the chosen plate or bowl the food is arranged, almost sculpted, and delicately garnished before being served. The meal reflects philosophical as well as culinary attitudes.

Of course, the chance of being a guest at a traditional meal is rare even for the Japanese, but there is much Japanese food to enjoy beneath these lofty heights.

Apart from an early Chinese influence, Japanese cuisine has developed in a state of isolation. Its style is unique. Buddhist beliefs, which forbade the eating of flesh foods, also influenced their diet and the main ingredients were rice, vegetables, pickles, seafood, soya-bean products and fruit. It is ironic that nowadays when this type of diet is highly recommended by nutritionists, the Japanese are eating more meat, dairy products and what must be the worst, most lifeless white bread in the world. The McDonald's Hamburger Bar in Tokyo is reputed to have the highest turnover in the whole chain.

At a Japanese meal individual dishes are served in small amounts but in greater variety than in the West. They are all served at the same time rather than in courses and the order in which they are eaten is a matter of personal choice. Dishes are classified according to the way they are cooked rather than by their main ingredient. At an elaborate dinner six or seven classes may be served.

Mushimono are steamed foods, of which a favourite is *chawan-mushi*, a custard-thick soup garnished with morsels of fish or vegetables. *Yakimono* are grilled foods and the most popular way of cooking fish. The shape of the fish is retained during grilling by threading skewers along its length. They go in and out of the body to give the impression that the fish is swimming. The best *yakimono* is prepared over glowing charcoal. *Agemono* are deep-fried dishes, of which *tempura* is the best known and loved. The finest *tempura* is made from a feather-light batter in which the very freshest shellfish, pieces of fish fillet or carefully cut vegetables are dipped. They are then deep-fried at just the right temperature and for just the right time. Golden brown and very hot, the *tempura* is served with a soya sauce and dipped in a *daikon* (Japanese radish) sauce, and garnished with slices of ginger and perhaps fresh lotus root. *Nimono* is food simmered in water or some other liquid such as *saké*. Thin slices of fish or meat are often cooked in this way. Diners pick the food out of the simmering liquid with their chopsticks. The cooking liquor is later supped out of a bowl like a soup. Other classifications are *sashimi*, in which pieces of very fresh raw fish are served with *wasabi*, a green Japanese mustard; *sushi*, vinegared rice patties topped with a variety of foods, particularly raw fish, and *nabe-mono*, which are one-pot meals such as *sukiyaki*.

Most Japanese meals are normally accompanied by *miso* soup and are always served with rice. *Miso-shiru* is a very popular soup, which is also served for breakfast. Its base is a fish stock, made from the bonito, which is sold in dried flakes in every food shop in Japan. This stock is then flavoured with *miso* paste. Floating in the soup are small squares of *tofu* and strands of seaweed or finely chopped vegetables. In the Japanese manner the soup is slurped with gusto from the bowl while holding back the solid bits with one's chopsticks. Rice is eaten with every meal including breakfast. *Han*, the Japanese word for rice, is given the honourable prefix *go* and rice is referred to as *go-han*, honourable rice. The rice at a meal is usually eaten last rather than as an accompaniment to other foods. The Japanese will eat two or three bowls of it. Strangers to Japanese food do not understand this and sometimes observe that a Japanese meal is not filling. In fact the rice is the core of a meal.

Apart from rice, noodles made from buckwheat and wheat flour, the three soya-bean products – *tofu, miso* and *shoyu* – and seaweed are the basic Japanese foods.

The Japanese eat noodles almost as often as they do rice. One of the great delights of being in Japan is to eat a bowl of noodles in one of the inexpensive noodle restaurants to be found in even the smallest village. The Japanese eat their noodles quickly with lots of slurping noises and 'aahs' of contentment. The way to do it is to lean over your bowl and start feeding the noodle strands into your mouth with chopsticks. Once started, you then suck the remaining length of the noodles out of the soup stock in which they are floating. After the noodles are eaten, take the bowl to your mouth and slurp out the residual soup or broth.

Tofu, better known in Chinese restaurants as beancurd, is made by soaking and grinding soya beans. The liquid extracted from the resulting mixture is then curdled. This is pressed into slabs to produce soft-textured, delicately flavoured, pale cream *tofu*. It is sold the day it is prepared. Most Japanese towns and villages have their own *tofu*-maker using traditional methods of manufacture. If you get the chance to visit one, do so. In Kyoto I passed a *tofu*-maker's workshop by chance. He was happy to let me stand and watch. He was intrigued that I should find what was to him such a commonplace activity so fascinating. *Tofu* has been described as Japanese cheese and it is used in some of the ways we use cheese, but *tofu* contains no fat and has more protein and vitamins than cheese. It is now being promoted in America as 'the food of the future'.

Miso is made by fermenting soya-bean paste in wooden casks for two or more years. By adding extra ingredients such as barley or wheat grains, different flavours ranging from the mild to the powerful are produced. *Miso* is rich in vitamins and protein. It is delicious in soups, sauces and marinades and keeps, unrefrigerated, almost indefinitely. *Miso* is available in the West. *Miso* soup is particularly nutritious and easy to digest for people who are convalescing or suffering from an upset stomach.

Shoyu is Japanese soya sauce which is traditionally made from naturally fermented soya beans. It is readily available in Japan and the West. Nowadays, unfortunately, much of the liquid described as soya is really an artificially flavoured cocktail of chemicals. It is best therefore only to buy soya sauce which is clearly labelled 'naturally fermented'.

In Japan seaweed as a foodstuff is commonplace, and its use is taken for granted. In fact *kombu* seaweed is packaged in fancy boxes and given as presents by appreciative guests when they go to dinner. As with land vegetables, the environment of the area in which the seaweed grows affects its quality and taste, but seaweed is usually rich in vitamins and minerals. Apart from its nutritive value, it is very useful as seasoning, and this is the way seaweed is most often used in Japan. *Nori, hijiki* and *kombu* are the most common types of seaweed. *Nori* seaweed is dried, pressed into sheets and wrapped around rolls of rice to make *norimaki sushi*. Crumbled over rice or soup, *nori* adds a distinctive flavour. *Hijiki* is cooked with soya sauce and eaten as a side dish; it is also good in salads or fried with rice. *Kombu* is best known as a basic constituent of *dashi* or Japanese soup stock, but it can also be used to garnish rice dishes, to season vegetables, and in a variety of other ways.

The main seasoning and condiments used in Japanese cooking are surprisingly few because the cuisine depends as much on the natural flavour of good fresh ingredients, their aroma and their visual beauty as on added flavouring. The main seasonings used, apart from *shoyu, miso* and seaweed, are *goma*, which is a mixture of toasted and crushed sesame seeds and salt, *mirin*, a sweet fortified wine similar to sherry, ginger root, *togarashi*, a blend of several spices tasting like a combination of black pepper and cayenne, and *wasabi*, a horse-radish mustard.

Japanese Restaurants

A formal meal is very expensive but while in Japan the opportunity to enjoy the experience at least once should not be missed. Otherwise you can eat cheaply in Japan at an amazing assortment of restaurants and cafés. Two notes of caution. First, avoid the places in big cities that provide Western-style dishes; they tend to be expensive. Secondly, the Japanese love to eat out and appreciate good food, but they are also happy to pay high prices for an ambience and a location a visitor to the country may not enjoy. Before ordering a meal, always make sure that the price range of a restaurant suits you.

In the restaurant deciphering a menu and ordering what you want when you cannot read Japanese is greatly simplified by the common practice of displaying very realistic wax models of the restaurant's meals in showcases outside the entrance. The type of bowl or plate which holds the model indicates the national origin of the meal. Large bowls with patterns around the rim are Chinese; plain or delicately patterned bowls or lacquered boxes are Japanese; and flat plates hold European or American dishes.

The custom of using models originated after the Meiji Restoration in 1868, when Japan reopened to the world. It was devised to help the Japanese recognize the foreign dishes which were being rapidly introduced into the country. The wax copies are so realistic that I initially thought they must be real food that had been varnished. Smaller establishments all use the same standard models, giving the impression that the same chef works at all of them. There is a wax-model-manufacturing district in Tokyo called Kappa-Bashi. The *kappa* is a legendary creature with the ability to change its appearance. Tourists buy the replicas as souvenirs. The Japanese Tourist Board in their publicity literature suggest the models 'make excellent party jokes'!

Once seated in the restaurant you will be given *oshibori*, *o-cha* and *o-hashi*. *Oshibori* are small napkin-sized damp cloths. In cold weather they are hot and in hot weather cold. Use them to wipe your hands and face and then as napkins during the meal.

O-hashi are chopsticks. At inexpensive places they give you disposable unpainted wooden sticks. These are joined together at the top and to separate them you merely pull one stick away from the other. In better places you are given lacquered chopsticks. Japanese chopsticks are more pointed, lighter and shorter than the Chinese variety and easier to use.

O-cha or green tea is as much a part of Japanese life as black tea is for the British. It is the common offering in all Japanese restaurants. Tea is given to you when you arrive and at the end of the meal without your requesting it. It is always free.

One final point before describing the various types of Japanese eating establishments. On no account blow your nose in a restaurant. This is judged very bad manners. Retreat to the toilet if your nose needs blowing.

FORMAL TRADITIONAL MEALS

Ryotei offer traditional Tokyo- or Kyoto-style full-course dinners. *Ryotei* are found in *ryokan* (Japanese inns) or as restaurants in their own right. They occupy unidentified premises which from the outside look like traditional Japanese homes. An advance reservation is needed and sometimes a personal introduction as well.

There is an alternative to this style of formal meal and that is a *shojin ryori* dinner. This is a beautifully cooked and presented vegetarian meal served in the dining room of a Buddhist temple. Again, you will need a reservation. The locations of temples which serve such meals are available from Japanese Tourist Board offices. There is a particularly famous one in Tokyo called Sanko-in Temple which is run by Zen nuns. The abbess, Soei Yoneda, is a very talented cook. Reservations need to be made months in advance.

SOBA-YA (CHEAP NOODLE SHOPS)

This is one of the commonest types of restaurant in Japan and one of the cheapest. *Soba-ya* serve four basic kinds of noodles in soup with garnishing on top.

Soba noodles are long and light brown in colour. They are made from buckwheat flour. *Udon* and *somen* noodles are both made from wheat flour and are white in colour. *Udon* are long and fat like spaghetti, and *somen* are long and thin. They are sometimes served ice cold in the summer. *Ramen* are the fourth category. They are the more familiar Chinese egg noodles. The Japanese find it very difficult to say 'rrr', so when ordering *ramen* ask for *lamen*.

To order in a *soba* shop, recognized by the noodle dishes in the showcases outside, just stipulate whichever noodles you want. Garnishings vary, but it is easier to take pot luck than to try to specify exactly what you want. They normally consist of one or more of the following: thin slices of pork, bamboo shoots, finely chopped leek, hard-boiled or fried egg, a few shrimps, fishcake slices, a few peas, pieces of boiled ham.

RYORI-YA (MODERATELY PRICED CHINESE RESTAURANTS)

This is a simple Chinese restaurant which a Japanese family might visit for a cheap meal. They sell Japanese versions of regular Chinese dishes. Anyone familiar with Chinese food will be able to recognize a *ryori-ya* by the dishes in the showcase and be able to order something familiar.

KORYORI-YA (INEXPENSIVE TRADITIONAL RESTAURANTS)

Koryori-ya serve a small menu of popular Japanese dishes such as seasonal fresh fish and vegetables. They are also relaxed places in which to drink beer or *saké*. *Koryori-ya* are usually small, with a couple of semi-private rooms with *tatami* mats. They are perfect for a small, intimate, inexpensive dinner. A *shokuji dokoro* is a very small version of a *koryori-ya*, only seating perhaps six to eight people at a few tables in *tatami*-mat booths. *Koryori-ya* and *shokuji dokoro* are easily recognizable by their traditional Japanese look; they often have unvarnished sliding wooden shutters at the entrance.

SHOKUDO (CHEAP MIXED-MENU RESTAURANTS)

Small and inexpensive, the *shokudo* sell a selection of the most popular Japanese, Western and Chinese dishes. They always display the complete menu of wax models outside. *Shokudo* are very relaxed and suitable for people travelling on their own. They are popular with students.

SUSHI-YA (MODERATELY PRICED SUSHI BAR)

Sushi shops are the most atmospheric and distinctive of all small Japanese restaurants. They sell rice delicately seasoned with vinegar, sugar and salt, shaped into rolls, patties, balls and so on. They are topped and filled with slices of raw, boiled or marinated fish, egg omelette, vegetables and seaweed. They also sell *sashimi* (raw fish) on its own.

There are two basic types of *sushi*: *nigiri*, which originated in Edo, old Tokyo, and *oshi*, from Osaka. For *nigiri-sushi* the rice is shaped by hand and then a topping is placed on it. For *oshi-sushi* the rice, together with boiled or marinated fish, is packed into wooden moulds of various shapes and sizes and pressed. The block is then cut into smaller sections. The most usual mould is rectangular-shaped, giving square slices of *sushi*.

The most exciting thing about a *sushi* bar is that the chef prepares the *sushi* in front of the customers as it is ordered. The *sushi* chef is incredibly deft and speedy, and as well as making and serving the *sushi* he has to remember the cost of each person's assortment of orders. The comparative skills of neighbouring chefs is a topic of great debate among connoisseurs.

Sushi bars are places of geniality and friendliness and the chef, if he is to be successful, needs to have a big, warm and welcoming personality.

A *sushi* bar is easily identified by its wax models of rice patties topped with raw fish. *Sushi* is served either in lacquered boxes or placed on the counter in small saucers. Inside the shop you can sit up at the counter and watch the chef at work, or away from the counter on small tatami mats. The counter is the place where you can most easily choose your selection of *sushi*. At the side tables the order is normally for a fixed combination tray. In many places they now have a conveyor belt rotating around the counter. On it the chef places an array of different *sushi*. As they come around the customer chooses what he wants; the price is calculated from the number of saucers at his place when he has finished eating. For the tourist *sushi* bars are good places to relax and enjoy the food and the Japanese at their best.

NOMI-YA (SNACKS AND DRINKS BARS)

A *nomi-ya* is a small, basic local bar and can be recognized by the large red lantern hanging outside. *Nomi-ya* are more for drinking *saké* and beer than eating, but they do serve snacks. There are no hostesses in *nomi-ya* which are relaxing places in which to sit and take time over a drink.

KISSATEN (COFFEE, DESSERT AND SNACK SHOPS)

There are many types of *kissaten* ranging from traditional tearooms playing Japanese music to modern coffee shops playing jazz or classical music. They normally have exceptionally good sound systems. The desserts and snacks can be Western or Japanese. Tea or coffee is moderately expensive but once you have bought a cup you are welcome to sit for as long as you wish. *Kissaten* frequently offer a good breakfast for the price of a coffee, early in the day. This is called 'morning service' in English. Morning service is excellent value and a boon to the tourist on a budget.

O-BENTO AND EKI-BEN (MEALS ON WHEELS)

O-bento are everyday lunchboxes prepared at home or bought in local shops. *Eki-ben* are train journey lunchboxes. They are sold on train platforms, in and around stations and on express trains.

The boxes themselves are made from thin unpainted wood or, for the de luxe versions, lacquered wood. Inside they divide into neat compartments and contain such foods as *sushi* rice, grilled chicken, mushrooms, smoked fish, pickled plums, fresh and cooked vegetables. They are sold neatly wrapped in decorative paper and tied with string.

Each area of Japan has its own variety of *o-bento* and *eki-ben* containing a particular selection of food and one or two local specialities. At Tokyo station there are stands selling *eki-ben* from all over the country, which are delivered fresh four times a day. The Mitsukoshi department store, Ikebukuro branch, Tokyo, even holds *eki-ben* fairs in November and February when for a week they sell all the popular regional *eki-ben*.

For those not travelling by train, *o-bento* may be purchased from shops in towns and on the main highways at refreshment stops. Special *o-bento* for celebratory or romantic occasions are available to order in larger cities. For a night out at the theatre it is possible to have a *makuochi*, 'between the curtains', or interval *o-bento* delivered to the theatre door.

A final note of caution. Do not touch the *sando-ichi bento* sold at large stations. They contain regular squares of crustless white-bread sandwiches. They are anaemic, lifeless and taste-less.

SPECIALITIES

There are many restaurants in large Japanese cities which specialize in one particular food. The list is too large to mention even a fraction of them, but here are a few that are usually appreciated by Westerners.

Okonomi-yaki   Do-it-yourself restaurants in which the cus-tomer makes his own pancakes from a batter and ingredients he has selected. The tables are inlaid with hot plates. Good fun with a party of people. Filling and quite cheap.

Tempura-ya   Foods deep-fried in batter served with a dipping sauce. Moderately expensive.

Sukiyaki-ya   Do-it yourself, one-pot meals of various veget-ables and thin slices of beef fried at the table. Quite expensive.

Oden   Foods such as *tofu* cubes, hard-boiled eggs, pressed fishcakes, *daikon*, *konnyaku* and seaweed boiled together in fish stock. Usually sold from street stalls. Unless you ask for something different the vendor will give you a standard com-bination. Cheap.

Yakitori-ya   Cubes of chicken and chicken liver skewered on bamboo sticks and grilled over charcoal. Cheap.

Communications

TELEPHONES

Telephones are easy to use and there are picture diagrams inside the booths showing the dialling procedure. Pay phones are different colours depending on whether they are for local calls only or for local and inter-city calls. Small red phones accept Y10 coins. They are for local calls – Y10 for three minutes. Yellow and blue phones accept Y10 and Y100 coins; they are for local and inter-city calls. No change is given from a Y100 coin. In big hotels and post offices there are telephones designated for international calls only. Green phones are for use with prepaid cards.

International calls may be dialled direct or through the operator. To get the international information service dial 03 270 5111 (03 is not needed in Tokyo), for the international operator, dial 0051 in Tokyo and 03 211 4211 elsewhere.

Dial direct international calls as follows: 001 + the national number of country being called + area code + local phone number. The national number of the USA is 1; the UK is 44.

Travel phones   The travel phone is a service provided by the Japanese government to help tourists. If you get into difficulties or need information then you can use the travel phone anywhere in Japan and speak to somebody in English. It is used in two ways; as a free service outside Tokyo and Kyoto and as a paid service (Y10 for three minutes) within these two cities.

Outside Tokyo and Kyoto, find a yellow or blue phone (not a red one) or use a private phone. For a public phone, put in Y10 and dial 106, tell the operator in English, slowly and clearly, 'Collect call TIC', pronounced tee-aye-see. The Y10 coin is returned with the call.

In Tokyo and Kyoto, use a public or private phone, any colour. Put in a Y10 coin and dial 502 1461 for Tokyo and 371 5649 for Kyoto.

POST OFFICES

Letters addressed in *romanji* sent to Japan and within Japan should have the address printed in large bold print. This makes it easier for the Japanese sorter. To post a letter or card in Japan, take it to the post office and have it weighed. Post office clerks read *romanji*. Large post offices may be used as *post restante* addresses.

Business Hours

Banks   Open from 9 a.m. to 3 p.m. Mondays–Fridays, 9 a.m.–12 noon Saturdays, closed on Sundays.

Post offices   Open from 9 a.m. to 5 p.m. Mondays–Fridays with cash deposit/withdrawal until 3 p.m. Half day (9 a.m.–12 noon) on Saturdays. Small neighbourhood post offices close on the second Saturday of each month.

Department stores   All open six days a week at 10 a.m. Some stay open to 8 p.m. although most close at 6 p.m. on Saturdays and Sundays and holidays. Some are closed on Mondays, and others on Wednesdays and Thursdays.

Shops   Most open from around 10 a.m. Some close at around 6 p.m. while others stay open till much later. Many, but not all, in the central business district are open on Sundays and holidays.

Tips for the Visitor

1. If you plan to travel a lot by train, purchase a JNR rail pass at a Japanese Airlines office before you arrive in Japan. They cannot be bought in Japan itself.
2. When you arrive in Japan, go immediately to the tourist office at the airport and collect English-language maps, railway guides, tourist newspapers and any other information you may need.
3. If you have the opportunity, spend your first week in Japan in a quiet area and get acclimatized slowly.
4. Take a good set of waterproofs, walking shoes and an

umbrella. The weather changes all the time and it is unnecessarily limiting to be restricted by wet weather.

5. The Japanese are prepared to be very helpful to foreigners but they do not like criticism. If you must say something critical, preface it with constructive praise first.

6. Buy long-distance bus tickets at a bus station. They can be bought on the bus but are more expensive.

7. Well-known tourist sights are very popular with the Japanese. If possible, travel midweek and rest at weekends. In this way you will miss the crowds.

8. Buy a Japanese phrasebook and learn a few useful phrases. Pronunciation is not difficult and once you try a few words the Japanese lose their shyness and try out their English.

9. If asking somebody directions or for other help, choose a young to middle-aged man or woman or a teenage boy. Old people are shy of foreigners and teenage girls are often self-conscious with them. They become tongue-tied and shrink into the cover of their friends if approached by one.

10. Do not worry more than sensibly about the safety of your property or person. The Japanese are very honest. Any transaction you may have in a hotel, shop, taxi, etc., will be straightforward. Do not haggle or tip; neither would be expected or understood.

Tips on Tokyo

1. Before going to Japan contact the nearest Japanese National Tourist Office in your country (addresses on p. 185) and ask them to send you their tourist maps of Japan and Tokyo. The latter is excellent and lists main hotels, airline offices, travel agents, embassies, department stores, museums and art galleries, information offices, shrines, banks, temples, sports facilities and major districts.

2. If you do not book accommodation in Tokyo in advance, ensure you arrive in the city in time to visit a Travel Information Centre (TIC) office before 5 p.m. There is one at Narita airport and one in the city centre (addresses on p. 186). They will help you find a suitable place.

3. As soon as you arrive in Tokyo obtain, either from the TIC office or from any large railway station, an English-language subway map. This is essential.

4. Before deciding what to do in the city, get a free copy of *Tour*

Companion, an English-language newspaper for tourists, and buy a copy of *Tokyo* magazine, an up-to-date informative publication in English. Both these publications contain details of current events. Both are available at the TIC offices and large hotels. Large hotels also always have a good selection of English-language guidebooks for sale and also free information. It does not matter if you are not staying in one, it is fine to go in and browse around.

5. Tokyo is a very large city, but it may also be thought of as a series of small, connected towns, each with its own character. By visiting and getting to know each of Tokyo's major districts (or towns) separately, you will find the city becomes more manageable and easier to understand.
6. For taped information on current events phone 503 2911.
7. It is very tiring getting about Tokyo and there is also so much to see, so do not plan more than two or three visits to different places in one day.
8. If you plan to visit Kamakura wait until you get there to buy a map of the city. The local authority publishes a map which illustrates a fascinating walking tour of the temples.

GOING TO AND FROM THE AIRPORT

Narita (also called New Tokyo International Airport) is the departure and arrival point for international flights. Honeda is the airport for domestic flights and those scheduled by China Airlines. There are a variety of ways of getting to and from Narita, but the two I would recommend are by the Keisei Line Skyliner train or by limousine bus.

The Skyliner leaves from Keisei Ueno station in Tokyo (it is adjacent to the JNR Ueno station). The journey takes an hour and then there is a ten-minute bus ride to the airport. Trains operate about twice an hour between 6 a.m. and 8 p.m.

The only drawback with the Skyliner is that you have to take the subway from central Tokyo to Keisei Ueno station. Its main advantage is that you know how long the journey will take.

The limousine bus (just a regular coach but called a limousine for some reason) travels from Tokyo City Air Terminal at Hakozaki (Nihonbashi) direct to the airport. However, the traffic can be horrendous and the journey can take a long time. To be sure of not missing your plane you need to check in for the bus four hours before plane departure time.

Take the bus if you have a lot of luggage and plenty of time. Otherwise the train is the best. Do not take a taxi unless you are travelling on somebody else's money.

SHINJUKU STATION

Shinjuku station is said to be the world's biggest and busiest station. It is also the Tokyo station least well signposted in English. A visitor to Tokyo who masters how to cope with Shinjuku will be able to use the city's other stations with ease.

Shinjuku has two wings divided by two long parallel passageways, off which runs a maze of underground shopping parades. Both private and Japanese National Railways (JNR) lines run into the station. If it is necessary to change from a private line to a JNR line, then you have to pass out through a ticket barrier, find your next line and purchase a new ticket. This is not needed if you change lines within the same company's network.

To buy a ticket, find your line first and then use the ticket machine nearest the line entrance. If you purchase a JNR ticket, you cannot use it on a private line and vice versa. If you do make a mistake, and it is quite easy to do so since all the signs and instructions are in *kanji*, there is a refund office but it is not easy to find. If you do not know how much your ticket will be buy the cheapest and pay the excess at your destination. This is a common practice.

In Tokyo I passed through Shinjuku regularly. If I came out into the main body of the station when changing lines, I was constantly surprised at how many different and unfamiliar places I could find myself in. In this situation the thing to do is to take your time and wander around until you pick up a signpost in English to help you get your bearings. The ticket collectors at the barrier gates are also very helpful and used to dealing with bewildered travellers.

Avoid Shinjuku if you have a busy timetable, otherwise you can happily get lost for a while and enjoy it as a place of interest in its own right. On a rainy day Shinjuku is an especially good place for window shopping and people watching.

Tips on Kyoto

Almost opposite the main entrance of Kyoto station, across a wide busy road, is a TIC office. Here you can obtain free street and railway maps of Kyoto and any other help you may need. With these and just one guidebook (two complicate matters in my experience), work out what you would like to do. The city is big and it takes a long time to get across town, so do not plan to do too much. Where possible walk from place to place; you will find many unexpected and interesting sights and shops along the way. When you arrive at your destination, take your time and get your bearings. Have a coffee or tea and absorb the atmosphere before taking a closer look. Do not be afraid to ask for information even with just a few words of Japanese and some mime. It is surprising how much you can discover in this way. If you are short of time, take a taxi. The drivers are helpful and used to dealing with foreign tourists. The fares are reasonable and they are fixed by meter.

In the chapter on Kyoto I recommend Tani House as accommodation for low-budget travellers. The address and phone number are as follows:

Tani House
8 Daitokuji-cho
Murasakino
Kita-ku
Kyoto
Tel. (075) 492 5489

Useful Information

ESSENTIAL GUIDEBOOKS

J. D. Bisignani, *Japan Handbook*, Moon Pub., USA, 1983.
Ian McQueen, *Japan: A Travel Survival Kit*, Lonely Planet Pub., USA, 1986.
Teikoku's Complete Atlas of Japan, Teikoku-Shoin Co., Tokyo.
Japan Railroad Map for Sightseeing, Nippon Kokuseisha Co. Ltd.

All books are available in the UK from Nippon Books, St Paul's Churchyard, London EC2.

JAPANESE EMBASSIES AND CONSULATES

Britain   43–46 Grosvenor Square
                 London WIX OBA
                 Tel. 01 493 6030

Australia	112 Empire Circuit
	Yarralomla
	Canberra
	ACT 2600
	Tel. Canberra 733244
New Zealand	Norwich Insurance House
	3–11 Hunter Street
	Wellington 1
	Tel. 859 020
Canada	255 Sussex Drive
	Ottawa
	Ontario
	KIN 9E6
	Tel. 613 236 8541
USA	2520 Massachusetts Avenue
	NW Washington
	DC 20008
	Tel. 202 234 2266

JAPANESE NATIONAL TOURIST OFFICES (JNTO)

England	167 Regent Street
	London W1
	Tel. 01 734 9638
Australia	115 Pitt St
	Sydney
	NSW 2000
	Tel. 232 4522
Canada	165 University Avenue
	Toronto
	Ontario M5H3B8
	Tel. 416 366 7140
USA	Rockefeller Plaza
	630 Fifth Avenue
	New York
	NY 10111
	Tel. 212 757 5640

Japan
(main office)　　　Tokyo Kotsu Kaikan Building
　　　　　　　　　　10–1 Yurakucho 2-chome
　　　　　　　　　　Chiyoda-ku
　　　　　　　　　　Tokyo
　　　　　　　　　　Tel. (03) 216 1901

TRAVEL INFORMATION CENTRES (TIC) IN JAPAN

Open 9 a.m.–5 p.m. weekdays, 9 a.m.–12 noon Saturdays, they have English-speaking staff who are most helpful when you arrive in Japan. They will give advice on travel arrangements and accommodation. The centres stock lots of useful free literature. There are three of them, one in Tokyo, one at Tokyo airport (Narita) and one in Kyoto.

Tokyo Office
TIC
6–6 Yurakucho 1-chome
Chiyoda-ku
Tokyo
Tel. (03) 502 1461/2

Tokyo Airport Office (Narita)
TIC
Airport Terminal Building
Ota-ku
Tokyo
Tel. (03) 502 1461/2

Kyoto Office
TIC
Kyoto Tower Building
Higashi-Shiokojicho
Shimogku-ku
Kyoto
Tel. (075) 371 5649